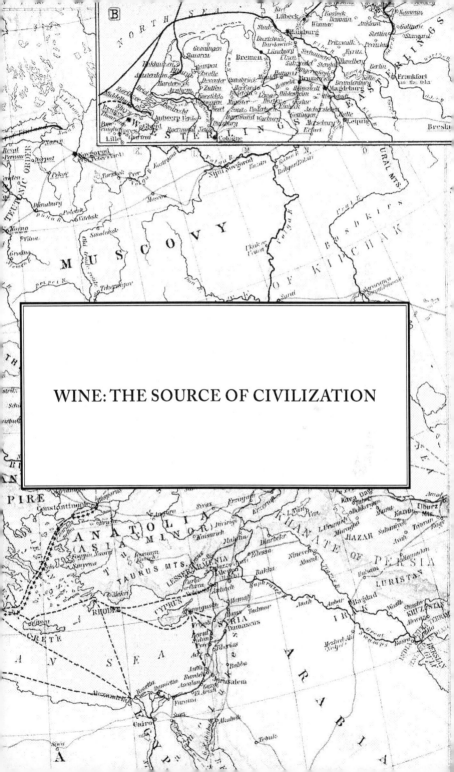

WINE: THE SOURCE OF CIVILIZATION

Other works by John J. Mahoney

The Year

Summer Tides & Cinnamon Thyme

Symphony of Seasons

Wine of the Muse

Every Bottle has a Story

Mystic Isle

Wine for Intellectuals

WINE

The Source of Civilization

JOHN J. MAHONEY

TORONTO DUBLIN NEW YORK MILMAY

John J. Mahoney can be reached through e-mail at j.mahoney@juno.com

ISBN: 978-172162782-0

1 3 5 7 9 8 6 4 2

To Paul Wagner, Michael Matilla, and
Lorraine Raguseo

To Paul Wagner, an expert in the world of wine, and a scholar of history and culture. When traveling with him through any wine region, he incorporates the local history into the study of the local wine. Thank you for all that you've taught me.

Also, to Michael Matilla, a man I've also traveled with through Spanish wine country. He too, sees wine as the focal point of each and every progressive culture, and always shares his knowledge. Thank you too for sharing your wine wisdom with me.

And, to Lorraine Raguseo who never tires in her enthusiasm to share wine knowledge. She understands that "wine is food" and wine is necessary for culture to advance into quality civilizations. Thank you for all that you've shared.

All three know that in wine, there is truth. *In vino veritas.*

CONTENTS

ACKNOWLEDGMENTS

Wine: The Source of Civilization, is meant to be a conversation about how our species migrated out of Africa, lived as hunter-gathers for thousands of years and finally, because it discovered the pleasure and life-enhancing qualities of wine, settled to plant vineyards, make wine, and then develop large cities and vast civilizations.

Continued encouragements from John Gartland, Maynard Johnston, and Gary Pavlis, who all read early drafts, provided suggestions, and helped in editorial review. They, and Henry Gorelick, Patrick Ruster, Don Graham, Walt Salvadore, and Vince Winterling provided me with the encouragement to do the tedious research, and numerous exhausting readings.

To Joanne J. Mahoney, and Erin C. Mahoney, who may complain, but never stop in their support and help when I'm writing, and to Sean T. Mahoney, without whose editorial knowledge and suggestions, I'd quickly fail, I say, "Thank you".

Lastly, to all the members of the *Dionysian Society*, the oldest and most refined wine organization in the world, all my friends in the *Society of Wine Educators* who have shared their wisdom, and to all the members of the *American Wine Society*, like two-time President Frank Aquilino, and President Joe Broski, I say, "Thank you".

To wine makers like Al Natali of Natali Vineyards, Jack, Charley, and Brian Tomasello of Tomasello Winery, Larry

Sharrott of Sharrott Winery, Jim Quarella of Bellview Winery, Jack Cakebread of Cakebread Cellars, BJ and Brock Vinton of White Horse Winery, Lou Caracciolo of Amalthea Cellars, Darrin Hesington and Toby Craig of Cape May Winery & Vineyard, Janet Trefethen of Trefethen Family Vineyards, Todd Wuerker of Hawk Haven Vineyard & Winery, Randall Grahm of Bonny Doon Vineyard, Kevin Celli of Willow Creek Winery, Shannon Brock of Silver Thread Winery, and Chuck Wagner of Caymus Vineyards go a special note of appreciation for their willingness to share both wine and knowledge.

Like my last book, *Wine for Intellectuals*, I hope this book is also a work that every member of every wine organization will read, and use to further their appreciation of wine, because it was wine that was the source of civilization.

THE THESIS STATEMENT

Man did not settle from nomadic travels to build cities and civilization, and then develop wine. Mankind stumbled onto wine by accidentally tasting naturally fermented grapes, and then changed from being hunters and gatherers into farmers and ranchers so he could grow, produce, and enjoy wine whenever he wanted it.

This desire to have wine led to the building of civilizations and empires, and not the other way around as the general consensus teaches. Drinking wine, I believe, goes back before the Bronze Age, yes, even into the earlier parts of the Stone Age.

It was Voltaire, the French Enlightenment writer, who was born in 1694 and died in 1778, and was influenced by both Shakespeare and John Locke, who wrote, "I want to know what were the steps by which men passed from barbarism to civilization." Many historians have written about the history of art, the history of different religions, the history of political changes, the history of philosophy, and so on, but few if any have asked what common item led mankind out of the caves to build cities and prosper like no other animal. The answer is wine.

In Egypt, wine was reserved for the Pharaohs, the high nobility, and the priesthood. It provided a mystical, god-like enlightenment too refined for the masses that only drank beer. The desire to achieve this meditative state of mind lead our early ancestors to settle, plant grapevines as they expanded agriculture, and then build cities. "If it ain't broken, don't fix it", must go back all the way to our ancestor cave dwellers. Hunting and gathering worked well enough. It was only after experiencing the super natural effect that wine consumption provided, that Stone Age man sought a life-style change.

It was wine that was the catalyst that created civilization.

The legend most often quoted is the Persian tale on how wine was first discovered. It tells of Jamsheed, a mythical king, somehow related to Noah because it tells of him saving the animals by building a watertight camp for them. The Persian poet Omar Khayyam wrote, "They say the lion and the lizard keep the courts where Jamshid gloried and drank deep."

The legend says Jamsheed kept grapes in clay jars stored for future eating at his court. One jar was kept apart because it was foaming with bubbles, and may have been poison. A harem damsel, looking for release from her nervous stress and head pain tried to kill herself by drinking from the poisoned jar. Instead, she slept well and awoke refreshed. The king and his court followed suit after they learned of her experience, and then left grapes to ferment from then on.

This legend, taking place at the start of the Bronze Age, only supports my contention that wine was accidently discovered, and with most legends, like the epic of Beowulf for example, the events happened long before the tales were recorded. As to wine, it had to happen during the mid or early Stone Age to give legends like this very early one time enough to develop and mature before it was recorded centuries later. It also shows that mankind, from the very beginning, was seeking answers to why and how things happened, which led to the start of scientific inquire, and later, the development of civilization.

The problem was, even though I wanted to produce a very short work explaining how the major civilizations came about, I realized that we couldn't just view a few societies and trace back their beginnings. It seemed to me, after spending countless hours researching, that just the tip of the vinous iceberg began to show itself when reviewing wine's role in Western Civilization. All of mankind came through the same rite of passage, and then developed different social organizations after it discovered fermentation. Wine provided the wealth that was needed to build the first cities, and then empires.

The more we know about wine, the more we will know about ourselves.

–JJM

WINE: THE SOURCE OF CIVILIZATION

1

NOMADS VS. SETTLERS

From African Plains to Caves then Villages

Noah's Ark settled on a mountain in Ararat in the lower Caucasus mountains of what now is Turkey. In Turkish, *Buyuk Agri*, recorded in Hebrew as Ararat, is the area that is now between Turkey and Armenia, an area that reaches up to nearly 17,000 feet. According to the Book of Genesis, Noah was the first winegrower. It tells us, in chapter nine, that as soon as he let the animals disembark, he planted a vineyard, leading to the first account of drunkenness when he fell asleep naked in his tent. Poor Ham, who saw him naked, was condemned to be the founder of the lower level Canaanites population of humans while Shem and Japhet, who covered their father, sired the prosperous populations. Bigots even today still use this tale as justification for their prejudice. Michelangelo painted Noah in this scene depicting the famous hangover on the ceiling of the Sistine Chapel. Pope Julius II wanted his Cardinals to see it. Thus, the Bible supports the idea that wine came from the Caucasus area of Armenia, which at the time covered southern Georgia and part of Turkey.

Sir John Chardin recorded his travel notes while passing through Georgia on his way to Persia in 1686. He stated that there is no country where they drink more or better wine than Georgia.

More and more evidence shows that wine production first began in Georgia near the Black Sea.

However, the *Epic of Gilgamesh*, a Babylonian story far older than the Bible, also tells a tale of a great flood. Like all epics, it talks about things from a much older past, and records the heroes who lived way before similar events were recorded in the same way that Homer wrote about Troy and the Greek conquests that happen long before his own time.

In the *11ᵗʰ tablet of Gilgamesh,* we find it written that Upnapishtim, maybe the original Noah, built an Ark, loaded it with animals and treasures, sealed the Ark with pitch as Noah did, sent out birds, and landed on a mountain like Noah. Unlike Noah, he did not begin to make wine. That topic starts in tablet ten when Gilgamesh seeks immortality, finds a godly vineyard, and if he were to savor the wines from it, he would have achieved immortality. The poet says of the vineyard, "It bears rubies as fruit, hung with grape clusters, so lovely to look upon." Since most events in remote histories have some true historical fact lying behind the tale, it may be recalling how Mesopotamia, which had no vines, journeyed to procure grapes and wine. This may be the oldest surviving literature coming from about 1800 B.C.

The Babylonian tales of *Tabi-utul-Enlil* tells of a good man put to every possible test before being rewarded by their chief god Marduk. It is the prototype of the *Book of Job,* but this story too, most likely came from the even earlier Sumerians. *Ecclesiastes,* and the *Book of Daniel* can also trace their sources to Babylonia. Their epic Gilgamesh is far older than the more modern *Iliad* of the Greeks. Their references to wine come from a far earlier time period, as do the stories about great floods, and how the gods punished mankind for being sinful. While the Hebrews were held in bondage by the Babylonians, they learned the stories they later passed on to modern Christians and Muslims. Wine was much more taken for granted and noted less often than the magical stories used as a basis for theology that kept the slaves and common people in their places.

Modern education stresses expertise in a single field, and to appreciate my premise, one needs to superimpose a number of academic studies. History of course, Archeology, Anthropology, Literature, Theology, Oenology, and a few other courses to help see the wider picture.

It makes sense to say that after mankind settled into cities and built civilizations, he included wine making into his new lifestyle. We have accounts of wine making and drinking from nearly every Bronze Age society, and I will relate more of them as we progress, but we have no record of who first chipped a flint to make fire, or who first invented a wheel. Wine, on the other hand, did not have to be invented, grape clusters falling into a puddle, maybe a stony crevice, would ferment naturally from the indigenous wild yeasts making the juice less sweet but stronger in alcohol. It would be a most unpleasant drink, I'm sure, but it would still intoxicate, providing mankind an out-of-this-world experience, a heightening of the senses and a reduction of inhibitions and fears. The taste may have been terrible, but the effect was beyond earthly.

During the Bronze Age even China, from the Shang through the Chou Dynasties, used wine in their religious practices. China is now about to become a world player in wine; currently with the amount of consumption, and soon in total volume of production. Their early wines did not come from *Vitis vinifera.* It was 128 B.C. when General Chang Chien got seeds and vines from the Persians for the Emperor of China. This was during the Roman period of world conquest. The Chinese and even the Japanese word for grape is *budo,* which has its roots in the Persian word for grape: *buda.* Marco Polo noted that China made a great deal of wine, and that the Shansi Province had excellent grapevines growing everywhere. As far back as the 7th century the Chinese knew how to freeze wine and remove the frozen water leaving mostly alcohol. Meng Shen, in the 7th century, recorded notes on the two kinds of grape wine. One beverage was made by traditional fermentation, and the other by distilling the cuvée with heat that was always the stronger drink.

Another fascinating note from the 13th century states that grape wine from Muslim countries was sent to Mongol Khan in glass bottles. It may have even been distilled into an orange-colored liquor, but in any case it shows that wine, for centuries, was used as a major item of trade, and the best was savored by the upper classes and nobility. It is quite clear to everyone that wine was the major item of trade during the Bronze Age, and even back into the late Stone Age. Thousands of grape pips have been unearthed near Lake Geneva at an early Stone Age site dating back 12,000 years or even older. It seems that right after the last Ice Age, our ancestors became preoccupied with the grape. There's no proof of any fermented wine there, but it tells us that the hunter-gathers were looking to settle and possibility grow what they needed. My contention is that mankind discovered, not invented wine, well before the 8,000 years ago (6000 B.C.) that has definitive proof with traces of residual wine found by Archeologist and Anthropologist.

All the historical legends intertwine.

Greek mythology has tales of Dionysus that reflect the Great Flood that Zeus forced upon the evil humans. Only one family was permitted to survive, and their daughter, *Hellen,* left her name for the Greek race: *Hellenic.* Her brother Orestheus is said to have planted the first vineyard just as Noah did in the Judo-Christian tales. His brother Amphictyon was taught by his friend Dionysus, about the rites, rituals, and the making of wine.

All the academic studies quickly come together.

A few years back, Princeton offered a History course on line. There were the usual readings and writing assignments, but what made it so unique was the world overview. When reviewing the time of Marco Polo, we also covered, what was happening in Japan, Chile, and Peru, the North American Native people, and central Europe. The over-view tied catastrophes and progress together. The following year I studied Archeology in an online Brown University course, and the next year I did an Archeology and wine tour on mainland Greece as well as the islands of Crete and Santorini. I'd already been to Mykonos, Rhodes and Patmos. A few years prior to this, I'd visited Ephesus in Turkey, and later touring Bulgaria's coast on the Black Sea, and then Romania, I began to suspect a much earlier history for wine than I'd ever read about or had been taught. At every location, as a member of the Dionysian Society, International, I recalled the toast new members make when becoming a lifetime member: *"To Wine, To the Dionysians and To Civilization."*

I realized that wine was more than a luxury; it held religious power, was an antiseptic, and was an item that provided a boost to the spirit in a world filled with vast hardship and drudgery. Wine was valued and sought out as a trading item. All alcohol is a depressant, but wine's ethanol did not depress the spirit or ambition; it depressed inhibitions permitting freethinking and open conversation; it limited pain and lessened social restrictions. It was a source of freedom and our earliest ancestors, after accidently sampling it, began to look for ways to get more or make it themselves. If they wanted to repeat any experience that wine provided, they knew they had to stop being nomads who only hunt and gather their food, and settle in one location to grow grape vines.

According to Will Durant, in his *Story of Civilization:* Part 1, *Our Oriental Heritage,* "Civilization is social order promoting cultural creation. Four elements constitute it: economic provision, political organization, moral traditions, and the pursuit of knowledge and the arts." This 1,049 page work explains that civilization is an "interlude between ice ages", and at any time another ice age, or major geological factor could reduce or wipe out what we refer to as civilization. Durant explains that tropical heat with it "lethargy and disease" deter the development of civilization. I note that quality species of wine grapes don't grow there either. Even though mankind emerged from tropical central Africa, the first aspects of civilized society developed in cooler regions where grapes could be turned into wine.

"Culture may come from the security agriculture provides, but civilization suggests the city," says Durant. Civilization then, results from a human civility that early bands of humans thought of as refinement, a *civitas,* or city, and what it can provide. The Latin word *civilis,* stemming from *civis* or citizen, is the root for our word civilization. Both the word and the concept are relatively young. Our species roamed, gathered, and hunted for hundreds of thousands of years before our brains expanded and our bodies morphed into the Homo sapiens we are today. The grape vine was doing the same thing as it slowly developed into today's *Vitis vinifera.*

*   *   *

Now is the perfect time to reflect back on how young we really are. There's no way of knowing how long life has flourished on our planet, but we know that evolution moves slowly but surely. The Age of Dinosaurs was the Mesozoic Era and that time period is broken into three time spans: the Triassic was 245-208 million years ago. The Jurassic was 208 down to 145 million years ago. The movie *Jurassic Park* shows what type of animals existed then. Lastly, the Cretaceous Period was 145-66 million years ago.

Only after the asteroid wiped out most of these species did the tiny mammals get the chance to evolve and populate the recovering earth.

Compared to these time periods, even the last four Ice Ages are relatively modern. The first Ice Age, say many modern geologists was 500,000 B.C. Then a long Interglacial period existed for 75,000 years giving rise to many new animals and plants. The Second Ice Age was 400,000 B.C. followed by a 200,000 year Interglacial stage. The Third Ice Age occurred 175,000 B.C. followed by a 50,000 Interglacial period of warming once again. The most recent Ice Age, a time period when we know we had living ancestors, was just 50,000 to 25,000 B.C. All of civilization as we know it has taken place during this newest Postglacial stage.

The oldest known upright walking humanoid was from about 4 million years ago. We named her Lucy. Mankind stood up for protection, and survived better than all the other apes that scurried along on all four limbs. We could see over the savanna grasses, and hide before predators got us. Our small troops migrated seeking food and shelter. We can trace every race back to our African parents.

During the Interglacial time period before the Fourth Ice Age, Neanderthals had spread over most of the earth. They lived for thousands of years during the Old Stone Age when rocks were used as tools, but they were not polished or reshaped. Not until 100,000 years ago do we find improved stone tools designed to better fit into a hand. Our word "hammer" can be traced back to its etymological beginning where it meant "stone".

At about 25,000 B.C. we find the first Cro-Magnon societies. They had larger brains than Neanderthals, created more polished tools, and even added engravings and artwork on their utensils as well as on the walls of their caves. They fought with and eventually eliminated the Neanderthals as a species from the earth. We call them cavemen because that's where we have found most of their remains, but it's safe to assume they were hunter-gathers who continually traveled to find food. It just happens that some of their remains were preserved in caves.

It's interesting to note that our modern brains have a 1450 c.c. capacity, while the Cro-Magnons' brain capacity was 1590 cubic centimeters. Think of all the things they had to invent, construct, and design to survive during and after the last Ice Age. They didn't even have any wine to comfort the long icy nights.

It's very difficult to put together a time line from that period up to modern man deciding to settle in one place to grow grapes around eight or nine thousand B.C. We do know that about 16,000 B.C. these Cro-Magnons made pins and needles, and advanced tools from not only stones, but also from horns and bones, and that examples of their work have been found all over the world. They learned to use fire at least 40,000 years ago, and that the use of fire sparked human advancement, changed their food items, increased their life spans, and offered protections from animals who, even today, fear fire.

The Prometheus legends about bringing fire from a volcano may have begun just after this time period. You could ignite a stick to carry fire home without chipping some flint, or waiting centuries to strike a match. With advanced stone work, the use of fire, and possibly even having tasted wild fermented grape juice, humanoids, looking much like us, began the New Stone Age about 10,000 years ago. That's just a blink of the eye in the time line of human-like existence. What we've accomplished in just the last century is greater than all of the earlier advancements combined. I can't even imagine what advancements the near future holds. It has been the concept of civilization that has allowed us to advance so much, and it was our desire to savor and experience wine that led to civilized societies providing the time and materials needed for our advancements.

Every tale we have seems to have come from a time when men bonded together in larger groups to build villages than when their families and close friends lived in caves. Their leaders had to explain things to assert their wisdom and power. They told of the god Marduk mixing his blood with mud to form a man. The rebirth of spring evolved into a text where Marduk "gives back life to the dead," and how the first women had a plant of knowledge stolen by a snake. Snakes were thought to be immortal because they shed their skins, and seem to start their lives over.

Villages grew into towns, and these bands of former nomads then grew into cities where status, rules, theologies, and social customs developed that are now considered modern ideas. How little we know about our past, and how under-appreciated is the role the grape played in aiding mankind to make advancements. One thing is for certain; whenever and wherever wine was made and traded, art, literature, music, architecture, and science soon followed.

The Greeks say they got the alphabet from the Phoenicians who traded papyrus, the first paper, along with the wines all early people wanted. It was easier keeping records on papyrus than on the heavy Mesopotamian clay booklets. The Phoenicians got some of their symbols from Egypt. The Greeks reversed many of those early letters because they wrote from left to right unlike the Phoenicians.

Wherever wine was traded, records had to be kept. The oldest writing with an alphabet has been found at *Serabit-el-khadim* in the Sinai going back to 2500 B.C. Archeologists found a library with clay tablets in *Zapouna* in Syria. Because *Zapouna* was destroyed by at least 1200 B.C., we know that their writings using letters went back to at least the thirteenth century B.C. Nearly every example of the earliest writing shows business transactions including how much wine was traded. As winemaking flourished so did the new civilizations. Recall that historian Will Durant said that trying to find an origin to mankind's history eludes us, and the scholarship of history is a text that has to start in the middle. Ancient Persia, for example, has roots growing from the Medes. They were Indo-Europeans who settled in western Asia at least a thousand years before Christ. They came from the Caspian Sea area. The Greek historian Herodotus says when they fell under control of the early Persians, they left ideas for Cryus, and later on, for Darius to use.

We know the Persians drank and traded wine in larger and larger volumes as their empire grew. Also, it's noted that when deciding on serious deliberations, Strabo wrote in 7 B.C., that the Persians regarded the decisions made while drinking wine more permanent than any decision made while completely sober and less enlightened as the Medes had done.

Wine was at the heart and soul of the largest empire the world had ever seen until the much later Roman experience. Wealth from their wine trade created this early civilization.

2

MASTERING THE GRAPE

Stone Age to Bronze Age

The beds of grape pips tell archaeologists that clusters were probably crushed, somewhat filtered and fermented into wine. Maybe the first of all cities built by man may have been *Catal Hüyük* in Turkey. Excavations have carbon dated grape pips back to 7500 - 5000 B.C. in Turkey, Syria, Jordon, and Lebanon, and the oldest dated back to 8,000 B.C., the late Stone Age, in the Republic of Georgia. The pips not only reveal their age, but their shapes can tell if they were from wild species or cultivated grapes. They proved that viticulture was among one of the first civilized acts of mankind after leaving a life of hunting and gathering to settle down to grow food, domesticate animals, and start building civilizations.

The land below the Black Sea was called Anatolia; Armenia was East of Anatolia and Georgia Northeast of Armenia between the Black and Caspian Seas. The entire area was covered in wild grape vines growing up trees, over huts, and among other plants. About 40 types of these grapes fit into the *Vitis* genus. The best one for making wine, *vinifera*, which means wine bearing, was soon noticed. *Vitis aestivalis* or summer fruiting vines, *Vitis riparia* or along riverbanks, and *Vitis rupestris* meaning rock loving were all related grape vines. Soviet archaeologists have evidence showing wild vines modified into cultivated vines dating back to the end of the Stone Age or 6,500 to 5,000 B.C.

Researchers very recently found wine residue on pieces of a broken jar from Neolithic times on a site in Georgia dating back to 6,000 B.C. This finding moves back the oldest evidence on Late Stone Age people drinking wine by a thousand years. It seems they made and stored wine in large 300 liter clay jars in a settlement just 30 miles from where Georgia's capital of Tbilisi stands today. The researchers found grape pollen, grape starch, and even the remains of fruit flies from the Neolithic period. Stephen Batiuk of the University of Toronto stated that alcohol played an important role in these early social groups. "Wine is central to civilization," Batiuk said for a Reuters report. Wine traces were found in eight clay jars, some decorated with grape clusters. Because of the residue chemicals, it seems that the wine was made with the berries, stems, and seeds fermented in the same vessel. This find actually out-dates the Chinese alcoholic blend of rice and honey dating back 7,000 years.

Grape vines are prolific and were growing everywhere. The last Ice Age reduced their territories to temperate latitudes from the Caspian Sea west into Europe. None survived below or above those areas. Grapes are like holly trees, willows, and other plants that have male and female flowers. The female plants produce the fruit. Hermaphrodites, plants with both male and female flowers, produce fruit, but less fruit than full female plants. As Stone Age man settled in one area to raise plants and domesticate animals, they would obviously select the female plants to grow grapes. Without the males, the female vines stopped producing grapes, and only after careful selection did our ancestors cultivate the hermaphrodites that feature the trait that now-days separates wine producing grape vines from wild vines.

Our ancestors were very observant; they had to be to survive. We seem to be losing this observational skill in our modern world. The stem-less wine glass is an example of modern man's decline of observation, and his failing to observe the different shades of color leading to the fading of his appreciation of the subtle things in life.

Today, botanists list *sylvestris*, or wild woodland vines, and *sativa* or the cultivated vines, as subspecies of *Vitis vinifera*. The grape pips found in Georgia among some late Stone Age settlements were *sativa* types of *Vitis vinifera* showing that wine was being made there seven to eight thousand years ago, and due to the fact that selections had to be made and improved each growing season, it was most likely, longer than that. Because of the rate of progress back then, I'd guess that it was at least 8,500 years ago, and possibly even 9,000 years ago that mankind started making wine. If so, wine is indeed the source of civilization.

The exposure to wine led to the growth of settled developments. Persia grew grape vines and they flourished very early; Mesopotamia had no vines so they had to trade for it. They used the Euphrates River as their trade route. Anatolia was their source for copper to make bronze, as was Cyprus and the island's name itself is taken from their term for copper. Tin is the other medal needed to make bronze, but there is no record of where it came from. Bohemia and Britain are possibilities. The Cornwall tin mines in Britain go back further than recorded histories, so it's possible that wine found its way to Britain in exchange for tin. In any case, the more that wine was used and traded, the faster these ancient civilizations grew.

The Phoenicians, who evolved out of the older Canaanites, expanded trading all around the Mediterranean with wine and grapevines being a priority item. They invented the alphabet, a word taken from the first two Greek letters, Alpha and Beta, and founded a series of trading cities all the way to Cádiz in southern Spain and Carthage in north Africa. The Greeks by then had vines planted abundantly, and they soon followed the Phoenicians in exporting grapevines around the Mediterranean. Commerce flourished. In 1987 A.D., a merchant ship, which sank around 1400 B.C. was found off the coast of southern Turkey with copper, tin, pottery, resins, blue glass, and wine all for trading purposes.

Luxor, the ancient capital in the Sahara, was the greatest city in the world at the time. Homer called it, "the hundred-gated Thebes" and it, even today, is filled with evidence of how important wine was to Egypt. During my Nile River tour down to the African highland of Nubia, I visited the Valley of the Kings and confirmed the idiom that "we know everything and nothing about Egyptian wines." Because the Egyptians recorded everything about growing, making, cellaring, vintage dating, even appellations, but nothing on how it tasted, we have an abundance of what they did without any idea of the final product's taste.

When King Tutankhamen's tomb was opened in 1922 by Howard Carter, the renowned Egyptologist, he recorded what was left there for the 19-year-old king to take with him into the next world. Sealed amphora, 36 of them, were labeled with the names of the areas the wines came from. Twenty-three of these wines were dated "year 4, 5, and 9" and one was dated the "year 31," far older than the dead king. This proves that they aged some of their better vintages, and must have enjoyed selected mature wines. The production, quality, and value of wine had come a long way since its first interaction with mankind during the Stone Age.

The *Vitis vinifera pontica* vines sourced from the Caucasus, where the earliest men cultivated and improved them for winemaking, were carried by the Phoenicians from today's Lebanon all around the known world. *Vitis vinifera orientalis* came directly from the Lebanon region and today, can be traced in Europe to the *Fendant* grape of Switzerland, and the *Gutedel* grape of Germany, also known as *Chasselas*, in northeastern France.

The vines from the Nile region make up another subspecies called *Vitis vinifera occidentalis,* which is thought to be the ancestor of most of our red varieties of wine grapes that we grow today. Most of the artwork found in Egyptian tombs shows black grapes and black juice flowing from their fermenting containers.

They depict treading the grapes in much the same way as it's still done in Oporto, Portugal. They developed a sack-press to squeeze more juice out of the skins after the treading was completed. The Egyptian word for this press is the same as the word for the tourniquet used to ring out their washed garments. However, with all the winemaking improvements the Egyptians made during this early Bronze Age period, they depicted their fermenting jars exposed to the sun. The late Stone Age Georgians fermented wine in similar jars, called *kwevris*, but buried them in the earth to keep them cool, and cold fermentations help retain more fruit aromas and flavors in the finished product. These *kwevris* were less like the clay amphora shaped, and more slender like the Roman *dolium* or the Greek *pithos* containers, both of which held wine and olive oil.

The scenes painted in Egyptian tombs depict the joyous occasions when drinking their wines. They show musicians, naked serving girls, ladies in conversation, wealthy couples and their pets all set in rooms with flowers, vine stems, blooms of lotus, and specific details on their drinking cups. Those beautiful cups were not made for water. No, wine was special and intended for important occasions. The Greek word, "symposium" means drinking together, and Athenaeus, the Greek essayist recorded, "They dined while seated, using simple but most beneficial foods and drinking only as much to be sufficient to encourage good cheer." Moderation in everything was the Greek theme for life, and Athenaeus wrote,

"In ancient times, the Egyptians conducted their symposiums with moderation."

Egyptian artwork shows that beer was for everyday ordinary people while wine was for the rich, the powerful, and the priesthood. The records show how special wine was.

During the fifth dynasty, in 2470 B.C., six appellations were registered along the Nile. Wine was also imported from Canaan and Syria. When they sailed to Byblos in Canaan to trade for lumber, they also bought wine. They needed the high quality cedars of Lebanon because palm trees are not worthy construction materials. Neither does palm wood make good barrels. The technology needed, and the skills of winemaking, were well developed by at least four to five thousand years ago. Egypt was in full production. Mesopotamia lies between the Tigris and the Euphrates rivers. They both start in the lower Caucasus Mountains, and then flow south to empty into the Persian Gulf. Cities like Kish and Ur, where they first used writings marked into wet clay to record production and sales, have left an artifact showing their ruler being toasted with cups of wine. The Sumerians who settled there came down from the north, down from near Georgian wine country, and they made pictograms of the things they highly valued. One such tablet shows a grape vine with its distinct leaf. Even though wine was made in the Mesopotamian regions, they still imported the northern Armenian vintages. It's assumed that local wines were for the peasants and slaves, and the higher quality, older regions of production wines, were for the priest and nobility. Just as with today's wines, the areas that have been making it the longest have perfected the techniques, and planted the best-suited varieties to make the better wines.

The Kingdom of the Hittites, Anatolia east toward Armenia, covered what's now eastern Turkey. It was the major source of copper as well as wine. Their civilization celebrated wine. We know this because of their magnificent drinking vessels. Cups of carved gold, and also their chalices were so beautiful that even the Greek craftsmen sang their praises well into the fourth century B.C. The area produced some of the world's greatest wines. Even today, Turkish Muslims still keep state vineyards at Elazig near the Euphrates just a few hundred miles south of Ararat, where Noah planted his first vineyard.

The most famous city in Mesopotamia was Babylon built by Hammurabi who is famous more for his code of laws and hanging gardens than anything else. It was the Hittites who eventually destroyed Babylon. They did, however, not destroy its record of "gardens filled with vines" that were producing grapes nearly 3,000 years ago. Hammurabi's Code also still exists written on clay tablets. It infers that women were supposed to be wine sellers, and even had their Queen Azag-Bau classified as a wine merchant. The laws show the importance of vineyards and wine. Clause 101 begins with, "If a vine..." and it covers the punishment for stealing, and even if someone's sheep strayed into a vineyard and ate someone else's grapes. It was wine that led mankind to settle and build cities, and it was wine that played so important a part of their lives that laws had to be written to protect it.

As I stated earlier, a full understanding comes from combining a number of different fields of study. History alone adds little to our knowledge of wine. Archeology and Anthropology must be included along with the recorded writings found in epic literature to paint the full picture. An abundance of evidence from the mid and early Bronze Age helps us draw conclusions, but common sense speculation is needed to fill in the history of wine's origin, and prove that it was the catalyst that triggered hunters and gathers to settle and grow grapes to make wine. Farming is seldom done alone. It calls for a larger number of people working together to plant, prune, protect, and then harvest a crop. Clusters of Stone Age people had to build dwellings near each other. A cluster of huts soon turns into a small hamlet, then a tiny village, and eventually, into a town from which cities grew.

For civilization to work, a division of labor had to be set up, and a hierarchy developed. A dominant personality became the leader; those with experience were the foremen, and the general masses settled into their labors for survival. The farming of grapes led to other plants being raised; then mankind was ready to build cities and empires leading to a civilized society of art, literature and order.

The grape vine became practical and spiritual. Vine cuttings have been found encased in silver sleeves and laid to rest with the dead as though they expected them to be replanted in the afterworld. They've been carbon-tested and dated to over 5,000 years ago suggesting that wine had already taken on a religious significance. This symbolic use of wine has been integral in Judaism for at least 3,000 years, and it continues through modern Christianity for the past two thousand years.

Our earliest ape-like ancestors, migrating out of Africa, just left their dead behind as other animals did during their migrations seeking food, but by the post Cro-Magnon times into the full Stone Age, as mankind desired more out of life, and found one uplifting experience with wine, it also began to desire a continuation of existence, even if just spiritual, so our ancestors began to bury their dead, garnished with flowers, in more and more elaborate graves. A short time later, they added gifts to the graves to be used in a hopeful afterlife. Many of our modern beliefs, and even our use of wine, turns out to be not so modern after all.

Gathering was easy. Hunting demanded the use of our first tools. It has been taught that man uses tools whereas lower animals do not. That is not true. Apes use rocks to crush nuts; birds use sticks to help weave a nest. It is better to define mankind as an animal that *makes* and improves tools. Spears, bolas, arrows, traps, boomerangs, and clubs were human inventions used to procure game. Today our hunting is taken care of in slaughterhouses; the experience of seeking out and hunting is still found in children's games. Even the word itself, *game,* lingers on. As we pushed forward toward the first civilization, we developed speech, cultivated grapes, planted grain, and developed writing to keep track of it all. Wanting an easier access to wine lead our species to practice thinking and develop better ways to survive. Converting a pointed stick that punched a hole in the ground where a seed could be planted evolved into a hoe, and from a hoe into a plow, which meant more of a food supply permitting a greater population. As our numbers grew, family units blended into packs, then into tribes that built small villages. More growth necessitated building towns, and with more thinking, more agriculture, and less nomadic travel, the expanding population created cities. With cities came civilization. Civilization expanded barter and trade, and wine was among the first items to be used in trade, and also as a symbol of growing wealth.

The Phoenicians kept records of their wine sales on the papyrus they got in Egypt. They also traded this early paper with wine and grain around the known world. The Greeks, later on, took the name of the Phoenician capital Byblos, as their word for book or *biblos,* and from that we got our word for Bible. As the Phoenicians carried wine around the Mediterranean, they spread the use of the alphabet, which they perfected from the Egyptians, and then the Greeks shared letters with their later worldwide empire.

The people of Byblos thought they were the oldest civilization ever created, and they taught that their god *El* founded their capital at the beginning of time. They had no idea how far back mankind went, nor how far he had traveled over the globe. They, like every early people, had many gods. They traded wine to gain wealth to build temples and provide rich offerings to them. The Phoenicians discovered the Cape of Good Hope centuries before Vasco da Gama. They traveled outside of Gibraltar, and founded colonies where they planted their best wine grapes in Malta, Sicily and Sardinia, then Corsica and north to Marseilles. They spread the grape-growing, and wine making techniques to Greece, Spain and Italy. They enslaved the locals in Spain and made them labor in mines for silver and gold just as the later Spaniards would do to the peoples of Mexico and Peru.

The Semitic people of the southern Middle East progressed faster than the northern Indo-European tribes that had far more to contend with for survival during the Ice Ages. The Semites were called *Semites* because they were thought to be descendants of *Shem*, Noah's legendary son whose family, it is written, were wine drinkers.

*   *   *

Whether it's Darwinian evolution, a biblical Stone Age Garden of Eden, or a combination of both, it was wine, not any forbidden apple that motivated our species to build civilizations. Before we could build societies, we had to master the grape. *In vino veritas* means, "in wine there is truth." That is the toast all

Dionysian Society Members still make when they are about to share their wine along with their wine knowledge. May we always continue to learn.

3
WINE'S ROLE IN ANCIENT SOCIETY
Bronze Age to Iron Age

Near the end of the 5th century B.C., Thucydides wrote as Athens' most famous historian, "The population around the Mediterranean began to rise from barbarism when they mastered the ability to cultivate the olive and the grapevine." He was telling the people that it was wine that had brought mankind out of the Stone Age and into the Bronze Age, and what was for him, modern times. No mineral or gem had ever made an equal impact as had wine.

Wine always goes hand-in-hand with culture, religious rites, marriage, and festive events. From the Bronze Age to today, its moderation has been stressed, but its quality has constantly been degraded. During the 1950's of the twentieth century A.D., terrible wines, fortified and sugared, were promoted to the less educated. Today, cheap wine is dyed blue, sold in cans for chugging, and poured off in volume from kegs. Whenever you don't study the shades of color a wine has, and savor its aromas before sipping, it's the alcohol you desire, and not the experience of enhancing food and enjoying the many complex experiences that the grape has to offer. It's always been this way, and about once every decade, some novel wine-based product is promoted to the unsophisticated. Back around 650 B.C., the Greek colony on Sicily created a drinking game called *kottabos*. It spread back to Athens and proved that as some people use wine to imitate the cultured, others could not help but degenerate into a tasteless hoard of drunkards. The *kottabos* game involved a tall bronze stand supporting a small statue on top with its hand held upward holding a tiny saucer. Wine, and any remaining sediment, was flung toward the stature hoping to knock off the higher and smaller saucer so it would fall and dislodge a larger disc. Of course it made quite a mess. Servants or slaves were necessary to the game for cleaning, just as necessary as was the *kottabos* stand.

The late Bronze Age, 1200 B.C., overlaps the start of the Iron Age beginning around 1000 B.C. During this transition, and again during the more recent Dark Ages, mediocre wine was used not to promote civilization, but as a drug to withdraw from the stresses their modern societies had created. Our concern is, as it should be, with the positive improvements in wine and the cultural, scientific, and the advancement of civilization that was encouraged by the desire to enjoy the pleasures of wine.

The Greek historian Herodotus described the wonders of what was to him, ancient Egypt. Here is a good place to quote the old Arab proverb, "All the world fears Time, but Time fears the Pyramids." Egypt lingers back to the mid-Stone Age. As they built their civilization, Durant quotes Maspero who recorded the old records, and found notes on what Egyptians ate and drank. He said that the rich, nobility, and Pharaohs drank wine while the peasants drank barley beer. The Arabic word *fellah* or peasant comes from their word *felaha* for plough, the tool peasants used. Four hundred years before Christ, Egypt had a population of at least seven million people with a quarter of them highly ranked and all wanting wine. The grape and its byproduct were a source of the wealth needed to build such a long lasting civilized society.

By the mid Bronze Age, one amphora of wine could be traded for one slave in Gaul, which was the territory that Caesar broke into three parts: *Gallia est omnis divisa partes tres,* as stated in the opening of his recorded seven-part story called, *Gallic War*: "All of Gaul is divided into three parts…" Germany, France and Britain. It was written in 58 B.C. when life was very cheap and wine was valued quite highly. It's thought there were far more slaves than amphora of wine. The Greeks, the Etruscans, and the Phoenicians all spread their civilizations and knowledge with each narrowly overlapping the others. All traded wine into what is now Europe, and all three groups sought tin from Brittan to add to their copper for their bronze weapons and artifacts. In 1952 a seven-foot tall wine bowl that held 1,200 liters was found in a Burgundian tomb at Vix. Theories differ as to where it was made. Some say Sparta, others confirm a Greek influence, but most believe the Etruscans of central Italy made it, carried it into Gaul, and bonded their trading relationships with it. It confirms that even then, the French loved their wines even before they were French, and long before they began to produce any quality vintages themselves.

Wine and olives were accepted everywhere they were taken. Grape vines and olive trees can easily be planted and produce well in land much too poor for planting grain or fruits. People ate better, and wine and olive oil helped prolong their lifespan. Populations grew, and cities became larger and wealthier. By 2000 B.C., Crete was a leading trader and a political power. Five centuries later, around 1500 B.C., mainland Greeks, the Mycenae people, surpassed the Minoan society of Crete in power, trade and influence. They moved more and better wines. Their famous leader Agamemnon, who led the fight against Troy, joined with Nestor of Pylos for the War. Nestor kept a 6,000 liter wine cellar all in jars called *pithor*. Homer gave us details about where they sourced wine for the troops, and notes Lemnos as the island with the most amounts of wines available for the army. It's only 50 miles west of Troy in the Aegean Sea, or the "wine-dark sea" as Homer called it. Troy's wine came from Phrygia, which was further east and deep in Asia Minor toward Turkey's Taurus Mountains where archaeological evidence reports that wine was being made 9000 years ago. Homer also described Achilles shield. It depicted a vineyard loaded with grapes made in gold with black branches supported by poles of silver during harvest time. The shield's edges were crafted with young boys and girls carrying baskets of grapes. Achilles, a major hero of the epic, carried a symbol showing the importance of wine even into battle. Homer also has Odysseus using wine to escape the Cyclops by getting him drunk with the strong Maronean wine, much stronger than the weaker Sicilian vintages that the Cyclops usually drank.

Wine can be a curse as well as a blessing thought some of the early Greek philosophers. Plato, for example, thought boys under 18 years old should not consume any alcohol. Why mix fire with fire he explained. Plato went on to explain that by 30 years old, drinking in moderation was fine, especially when an evening called for a symposium, which is "drinking together" while conversing about the nature of life. At 40 years old, which was considered old age at the time, Plato said that wine was a "cure for the crabbedness that comes with old age."

Aristophanes, the comedy writer, said, "Why ponder now; it's when men drink that they thrive." Aristophanes isn't taught as much anymore as we dumb-down our educational process and wait for the next Dark Age period.

Athenaeus, an Egyptian Greek, wrote "The Deipnosophists" during the 2nd century A.D. that recorded conversations about wine and food from 24 of the best-known scholars on gourmet ideals. The title translates as "The Knowledgeable Diners", and from it we can learn how the wine snobs of the day were acting. Hippocrates, on the other hand, provided specific details as how to better enjoy good wine. Born on Kos, a small island, in 460 B.C., he recorded all his medical remedies. As the father of medicine, he said newer wines are more nourishing. We learn that they made wines sweeter by doing only a partial fermentation. Hippocrates recorded that these sweeter wines go less to the brain, and cause less heaviness in the head. He also stressed that wine be neither too warm, saying it would make you an imbecile, nor too cold which can lead to convulsions. He would have loved today's wine glasses with a stem so your hand neither chills, nor warms the wine by its contact with the bowl.

Socrates, possibly the most brilliant Greek thinker, said that wine revives our happiness, and as we get old, wine is oil to the fading flame of life. Socrates taught that wine tempers our spirit and sets our minds to rest, and when drunk in moderation, wine perpetrates no rape upon our ability to reason. Every lover of wine should study Socrates because he basically confirmed the premise that civilized men came about through the evolution of winemaking ability, and its prolific production.

The less famous playwright Embolus won the *Lenaia*, six times. It was the dramatic competition and, writing in about 370 B.C., he provided ageless wine wisdom. One *kylix,* the Greek drinking cup, is consumed to health; a second to love, and a third to a restful sleep. He says that a fourth no longer belongs to us but to violence. A fifth cup leads to uproar, a sixth to drunkenness, a seventh to injury including black eyes; the eighth cup will invite the police authorities. A ninth *kylix* of wine leads to biliousness and its gastric distress, and a tenth to madness. We've been warned.

More and more proof is being found all the time to confirm the thesis statement for this book.

On the Greek settlement of Sicily, wine making was thought to have developed sometime between 1350 B.C. and 1150 B.C. However, very recent discoveries and analysis of residue found in storage jars discovered in Agrigento, Sicily, show that winemaking can be confirmed back to just over 6,000 years ago. Scholars are continuing to research more of Sicily, and also Malta. Once they can determine if the wines were red or white, they can trace back into the sources of these grapes. The traces of sodium salts and tartaric acids that they found are compounds found in the winemaking process. The residue was found in a copper jar large enough to be used as a fermenting tank.

*   *   *

Whether analyzing the 8,000 year-old sites in Georgia, or researching Bronze and early Iron Age amphora that the Etruscans left in France, the most sensitive processes available are used. Liquid chromatography-Orbitrap mass spectrometry research on the making, serving, and drinking pottery found in all the research locations shows that these earliest settled dwellers had indeed developed a wine culture. These techniques have shown traces of basil, thyme, rosemary, and resin from pine trees, all available from central Italy's Etruscan areas, were added to the exported wines. Those additions would help hide any faults that developed in the wine as it traveled the long distances. This was a problem that continued to be a major concern right up to the late 19th Century A.D.

The Greek and Etruscan trade expeditions quickly replaced Celtic drinks made from barley, wheat, wild fruit, and honey with wine made from *Vitis vinifera* grapes. The "Indiana Jones of Ancient Wines," Dr. Patrick McGovern, is the Professor of Anthropology at the University of Pennsylvania Museum. He has confirmed the earliest dates of winemaking. Confirming that wine was in use before civilized culture, it's easy to conclude that wine, a food product that transcends all other foods, was paramount to developing civilizations.

During the century between 1200 B.C. and 1100 B.C., the Dorians, invaders from the north with very little known about them, devastated most of Greece and the surrounding Aegean settlements. It was a Dark Age for civilization. Writing itself was lost. The Dorians abused wine unlike the Greeks who drank in moderation. Their oppressive life styles could not last, and within one and half centuries, the Greeks once again imported wisdom from the east, began making iron instead of bronze, and put a new alphabet into use, one that we can still recognize today.

Euboea is the second largest Greek island, and it is from there that the Greeks built bigger and better ships with borrowed Phoenician engineering ideas. They sailed with grape vines to Cyprus, to Italy, and began to deal with the Etruscans who were thought to be descendants of the Trojan refugees. They founded

Syracuse in Sicily. Greeks from Rhodes founded Gela. Greeks from northwest Peloponnese settled Sybaris. Spartans settled in our modern Taranto inside the heel of Italy. Greeks from Rhodes founded Naples. Most of Italy from Lombardy south was known as the greater Greece or *Magna Graecia,* and much of this area's peoples called themselves, *Oenotria,* or people in the "land of staked-up vines."

Just before 300 B.C. Alexander III of Macedon conquered the entire known world, and even ventured into parts of India. I love his famous quote; "I am indebted to my father for my life, but to my teacher for living well." That's one the modern Dionysian Society members all try to follow. Because his armies drank wine and mixed it with water, they were seldom sickened in new areas, and could easily defeat armies who may have been too ill to fight as strongly as the healthier Greeks. The later Romans attributed their success in foreign countries, where the water would sicken them, to the wine they added to the water, or drank only pure wine. Ironically, for Alexander, modern toxicologist like Dr. Leo Schep of New Zealand, believe he died at just 32 because he was poisoned, possibly with the *Veratrum album* plant, of the lily family. It would cause a slow painful death, and it took Alexander 12 days to die.

We've learned about our ancestors from literature, which includes the histories, poetry, and drama. We can also analyze the residue found in the millions of amphora that are broken, empty, and even some still sealed examples. The Latin word for opening an amphora simply means to "scrape its top." The were closed and first sealed with wood, then cork, and then cork coated with wax or resins to keep out the air which they learned quickly enough turned the wine into vinegar. They learned how good aged wines could be after they figured out that it had to be sealed prior to storage and cellaring. It wasn't only the Egyptians who learned to love older vintages. Mankind was making progress when he learned to appreciate the complexities of aged wines that demanded contemplation as opposed to the instant gratification of simply big fruit and high alcohol wines.

It's believed that the Canaanites invented the clay amphora, and as the ancestors of the Phoenicians, it makes sense because of their vast travels, that they would expose them to Egypt and Greece just before or around 1500 B.C. These amphora were used both for fermenting containers and for storage. We know them today as amphora because it's a Greek word meaning "a vessel that can be carried by two people." They had handles on them, which the earliest Egyptian containers did not have. The Greek amphora held nearly 40 liters of liquid. The later Roman examples held 26 liters, which is just about three modern cases of wine, or 36 bottles per Roman amphora. Amphora were made in sections and fused together with wet clay and baked. The bottom was always pointed or rounded off with a ball-like knob. They needed a stand to hold them upright when separated from leaning against each other. The bottom served as a third handle, and made it easier to tip and pour from them. The pointed ends were placed into sand when being shipped to distant ports, and of course, they had to be tied together during the journey. The Greeks also shipped grain and oil in amphora, and later the Romans shipped fermented fish parts called *garum* in them. There were tens of millions of amphora made during this late Bronze Age period of wine development; so many that even today many of the Aegean and Mediterranean beaches are coated with parts of their broken remains.

* * *

As wine improved, so did the societies that consumed and traded it. The great Han Dynasty of China flourished as trade grew. This was the period when Chinese pottery became the most beautiful, and it was traded with empires of the Near East. It's recorded that the state took control and ownership of iron and salt mines, and the complete control regarding all transactions of wine sales.

China leaned toward a quiet and peaceful existence based on tradition, scholarship, and respect for their ancestors instead of working on scientific advancements. They were the first to burn coal; could make glass, but would rather import it; may have been the first to use a compass during Emperor Cheng Wang period of 1115-1078 B.C.; could figure π to at least six decimals, and designed a calendar with twelve hours and twelve months.

Their goal was to have harmony with the sun, the moon, and the earth. Only in modern times has China expanded its desire to consume, grow and make wine, even buy and run famous international wineries around the modern world. Today, its economy and trade has pushed it forward into a world power. It's very hard to decide the time-line for whether China's wine desires inspired economic and civilized growth, or that the need for wine grew after their civilization modernized. I think wine was the secret catalyst for Chinese advancements. We'll discuss this a bit more near the end of this book.

The same Tatars and Huns that destroyed the Roman Empire with a resulting period of long Dark Ages crossed the Great Wall, and ended all civilized concepts in China. These barbarians did not grow grapes. They stole and drank what they took from conquered civilizations that made and promoted advancements in wine, but they never built any civilization. A direct correlation between wine and civilization appears over and over again. Wine, it seems is always the catalyst that builds better societies.

*　　*　　*

At the end of the Neolithic era, a white race called "Ainus" entered Japan. Coming from Korea, and even further inland, a yellow Mongol people migrated to Japan at least 700 years before Christ. A third brown Indonesian group sailed in from the islands.

Their mixture evolved into today's Japanese.

The Japanese had little government, and almost no trade until the Portuguese wine and spice traders visited, whom they shunned, and then not until American fleets arrived in 1853, did Japan open itself to the civilized world. Again, it seems that where there's no wine, little progressive civilization develops.

Through the Bronze Age and into the early Age of Iron, it was wine that provided the wealth needed to build civilizations.

4

THEOLOGY & WINE

Wine's Role in Myth

The early civilizations, especially the Greeks, were excited about wine for more reasons than just economic and social ones. They explained it all through Dionysus and worshiped him. His biographical legends greatly influenced the later Roman Empire where he was known as Bacchus and Osiris in Egypt. We'll review the Egyptians a bit later; they had a brief period with only one god. In fact, legends of a wine god trace back just over 9,000 years to later Stone Age temples and religious sites in the first known city, *Catal H*üyü*k*, where a baby wine god is depicted sitting with Mother Earth in a similar manner as the Renaissance sculptors depicted Baby Jesus on the lap of Mary. The Greeks said that there was nothing new under the sun, and maybe they were correct.

Drama developed along side early religions, and in many examples, as a ritual for Dionysus. The first theater was built just below the Parthenon of Athens, and it still exists today. The symbol of drama, the two masks of comedy and tragedy, were first worn to help theatergoers distinguish the characters, and to help project their voices, megaphone-like, deeper into the audience. As wine created and enhanced the growth of civilizations, all the social aspects surrounding it grew also making it both earthly and spiritual. More than 13,000 Greek citizens would fill the theater by the Acropolis on the opening day of the Festival of Dionysus. These early Greeks made sacrifices to, and participated in social-religious rites for Dionysus, but their gods were not worshiped in the sense we think of in the services of modern religions. All the other gods were either feared or prayed to for help, but Dionysus alone became a living part of their lives. They partook his gift of wine; it represented him, and they became one with him.

The Romans, who called him Bacchus, developed the Bacchanalia, a multi-day festival that grew worst and worst into drunkenness and orgy until it was banned. Followers of Bacchus were accused, not unlike the early Christians, of acting and being un-loyal to the Roman government. Titus Livius, who was born in 59 B.C., and died in 12 A.D., was better known as Livy, the Roman historian. He recorded a story about how Aebutius' stepfather tried to gain his stepson's inheritance by disgracing his mistress Hispala. He forced her to attend a Bacchanalia where she might be sweep into the disgraceful actions where the drunken found no crime, sin, or pagan activity untried. The Roman Postumius was excited to gain this information, and used it at a meeting of the Senate to have them outlaw the Bacchanalia. However, the cult persisted and Julius Caesar eventually lifted the ban. Bacchus, who was the same god the Greeks called Dionysus, was the favorite god of the common man, and those in power knew very well how far they could go with restrictions on common behavior. Had the American political leaders been as sensible as Caesar, the decade of Prohibition, which funded all future organized crime, would have never taken place. Legislating morality has never worked. Education and gaining wisdom is the solution to society's problems, as the wine-drinking civilized Greeks taught us. The modern Dionysian Society holds no theology in their activities, just an intellectual appreciation of the qualities of modern wine, and all the art, theater, and music that surrounds it.

A 5th century mosaic from Paphos on the island of Cyprus depicts the infant Dionysus on his mother's knee with Ambrosia and Nectar, the divine symbols for food and drink. It is a scene quite like "The Adoration of the Magi." Diego Velazquez, who painted for the court of King Philip IV of Spain, painted Bacchus as a real human being living among the locals of Castile and Rhinelanders. Velazquez had him dressed as the satyrs where during their annual Weinfest. Every year in Spain, on San Pedro's Day in Rioja, thousands of people march to Mass at dawn, and as soon as it's over, the hordes of people, like ancient pagans, howl and sing, spray wine from their sheep and goatskin wine bags, and soak everyone with the local red wine. Under olive trees dating back for centuries, they dance and frolic in the wine-filled mud of the earth happy that Dionysus gave them wine.

In 392 A.D., Emperor Theodosius prohibited the ancient pagan cults. The Bacchus followers simply adopted the early Christian symbols as the Christians had borrowed from Dionysus' mythology. The infant Bacchus on his mother's knee, and even the depicting of halos that went back to Stone Age *Catal Hüyük*, mankind's first site of a civilized city. All of the Dionysus-like characters, Osiris, Bacchus, as well as more ancient gods, were all brought back from the dead, had a god for a father and a human mother. They worked miracles, and were persecuted at one time or another. Either our collective history or a desire to maintain our past, leads people to continuously intertwine legends with fact. Gregory Nazianzos, the Archbishop of Constantinople during the 4th century A.D., and Doctor of the Church, known in the East as Saint Gregory, wrote a drama called, "The Passion of Christ," in which he borrowed, and used entire passages from Euripides' play "The Bacchae." This thesis is not a comment on organized religion. It is simply a comment and partial history on wine, as well as theology's wine-related effects on mankind's evaluation from a hunter-gather primate into a civilized homo sapien.

Dionysus' name, according to Pindar, is derived from the words for "Zeus", his father, and "Nysa", the location of a mountaintop where Dionysus was born and raised. Pindar wrote lyric poetry around 500 B.C., and of the nine canonical lyric poets, his writings are the best preserved. Pindar was confirming Dionysus' divinity.

Orphic beliefs dating back to the 6th century B.C. stem from the mythical poet Orpheus, who as Dionysus did, descended into the underworld and then returned, much like Persephone, who descends each year, and then returns bringing back life in spring.

Orphism had already considered spiritual salvation through Bacchus or Dionysus as the savior. Eating from the dead was a quite familiar idea at that time, and so was drinking the blood of Bacchus, which was his gift to mankind: wine. The Roman army held *Sol Invictus,* their sun god in high esteem, and with the help from much earlier ideas, they depicted him with a halo that early Christians borrowed to incorporate into their religious art. Even our modern celebration of a savior's birth is held right after the return of the sun from the shortest day of the year.

The Christians, in an effort to convert the Germanic tribes, chose their winter holiday for Christmas, just as Easter is a return from the dead spring rebirth event. We cannot escape our past legends any easier than we can negate wine from our social activities. Greek thought, and its wine practice, had spread east to Anatolia and toward India, and also to Egypt and remained so with Ptolemy and his writings. Then, Greek ideas spread westward through Italy as the Roman Empire began its rise to being the ultimate ruler of the known world, but by then, Dionysus' themes had already been accepted everywhere.

We think of Christianity as stemming directly from Judaism, and expanding in Rome until years later when Constantine made it the official religion to placate the population. He did that because the Christians were the best organized of the many cults populating Rome. However, let's not forget that the New Testament was not written in Hebrew, but in Greek. The Bronze Age Greeks offered brunt offerings to the gods as flesh brunt. Then they ate the meat as a supper with their gods. Christianity developed their symbolic sacrifice from Greek tradition, not from Jewish customs. The Greek word for god is derived from their word for smoke: *theos.* It's from the same root *thusia*, or "filled with god", and it is used in our word en<u>thu</u>siasm today. Over a thousand years prior to Jesus' time, the Greeks drank wine as a symbol of the blood of their gods in a sacrificial rite called *eucharistia,* so it's easy to see how the Christians' ceremonial worship is tied to ancient Greek sacrifices. Once much of this Greek influence was absorbed into Christianity, the Jews pushed it off as impossible to accept.

By the time Constantine converted, on his deathbed, the Christian religious ceremony shared bread and wine in similar ways as all the ancient ones had done. It is still done today with different levels of significances between a Catholic High Mass, and a weekly Baptist service. The first services held in Rome's catacombs also included fish, a symbol used by Christians even today, but the communal meal is just bread and wine. Even in Judaism today, they have wine restrictions stemming back to the ancient Baal worship as they restrict any Gentile from touching, or being in any of the winemaking process. Their kosher wines are a must for all their ceremonies, and it's interesting that proportionately more Jews drink wine in the USA than any other ethnic group. At the same time, they have the least number, proportionately, of alcoholics. Sociologists seem to think it has to do with their families initiating wine into their religious celebrations where drinking is always very moderate. Knowing that many of the wines used were very sweet, even cloyingly sweet, and not food compatible, helps to keep the volume ingested quite low.

Jewish dedication to wine is found throughout all their literature and their laws. Sabbath calls for a cup of wine to be shared by the entire family. One cup at circumcisions, two at weddings, and four cups at Passover presents the joy of wine into all acts of worship, but the Jews never could accept the levels of intoxication resulting from most of the ancient Dionysian cult activities. Every book of the Old Testament has a reference to wine except the Book of Jonah. We know that there are many wines that complement fish, but Jonah, not the whale, was the meal in that tale. It's good to recall that the followers of Moses, when they first saw the Promised Land at Canaan, said they saw an enormous cluster of grapes, a scene depicted in many artistic scenes. The psychic Joseph, who interpreted the Pharaoh's dreams, had seen vines being grown, and even Jesus called himself "the true vine". Biblical references to wine are very prolific.

We know that the Tribes of the Jews were taken into captivity to Babylon around 585 B.C. During this exile, they heard the older mythology that Babylon actually took from an earlier civilization, the Sumerians. These are the people who constructed the potter's wheel, and also provided the future basis of the much later Industrial Revolution. They invented the wheels for the first wagons, and wheels became the most basic tool of modern industry. These items were found in later Babylon, and even more recently in ancient Egypt. Their culture was expanded to the city of Susa in Persia. When those people were considered an ancient society, their priests tried to record their own history. They wrote, being the first people to produce writing, about their own creation from a fundamental Paradise where an enormous flood destroyed everyone because of the sins of an older king. The Babylonians kept the tradition of these stories, and passed them on to the Hebrews where they became part of their own traditions. Both Noah, and the Garden of Eden tales, seem to have begun their fundamental outlines with these late Stone Age, or early Bronze Age people when men first viewed wine as an important spiritual drink.

Nebuchadrezzar II was the famous villain recorded in the Hebrew Book of Daniel. They had temples to their chief god, Marduk, which very few of the Jews accepted. The famous Tower of Babel rose 650 feet, and was later noted in Jewish writings as the place where God changed all the languages. We use "babble" as what babies do, and think the word came from the Tower's name, but in reality, it meant the "Gate of God" in Babylonian. The Greeks, much later on, listed the Hanging Gardens of Babylon among their Seven Wonders of the World. They saw them as a civilization that traded wine and grew rich because of it.

The Babylonian clay tablets record lists of their kings back for thousands of years, and even though they most likely grossly exaggerated all the names, they did record Tammuz, and also Gilgamesh, who later on became the hero of Babylon's great epic poem. Stories of Tammuz were passed down for centuries, and later he became the Adonis of the Greeks. These heroes drank wine. Production and the trading of wine provided the capital to built such ancient places. Before Nebuchadnezzar, the famous Hammurabi set up his code of laws, the first listing of rules for any society. He even more importantly dug a canal to the Persian Gulf to foster trade, and irrigated nearby land for agriculture. They had to import far more wine than they could make themselves. It seems that wine was always at the focus of these early progressive civilizations.

*   *   *

The *Bacchae*, written by Euripides, was first seen in 404 B.C., on the stage Pisistratus had built in 530 B.C. The wine god was raised to prominence by 850 B.C., and officially confirmed in 582 B.C., when he was given three months a year as the top god's oracle at Delphi. Because the wine trade was so important, the evangelism of Dionysus expanded through colonies and commerce. Grape vines could be grown without irrigation, in poor quality land, even on high rocky hillsides, and stony valleys. Its end product could be used as a nepenthe for the depressed, as an aphrodisiac, as an anesthetic, and as a tonic to help raise the spirits of people living in a time when just to survive was a constant struggle. Wine became their savior. While the powerful and the strong were inspired by Apollo, the ordinary person looked toward Dionysus for comfort.

After the last great Ice Age, mankind was ready, and deservedly so, to start looking for more in life than just surviving. Men of the Early Stone Age must have related tales and stories of Ice Age heroes, just as Bronze Age accounts relate legends of monsters, floods, wars, and heroes from earlier eras. By the time of the Roman Empire, only 2,000 years ago, wine had promoted societies and civilizations where science and logical thought was beginning to replace the fables and fears of ancient times. This metamorphosis of mankind from animal-like hunter-gathers into thousands of settled city dwellers was completed. The only thing remaining was the improvement in vine selections, wine growing techniques, and winemaking skills. Before we jump too far ahead, let's confirm the special importance of the school of Dionysus.

The concept of Dionysus traces back for at least 9,000 years where he was thought to be the child of Mother-Earth herself. Between three or four thousand years after that, in Mesopotamia, the mother character name *Kubaba* appears. The neighboring Hittites sang her praises and celebrated *Sabazius*, her son, who died each year, and was then reborn. Further west into the Aegean, the people of Lydia sang her praises. Lydia was where the god of vegetation was first referred to as Bacchus, and sometimes *Bakhos*. Centuries before the time of Homer, Orpheus sang of Dionysus being the son of Zeus and Persephone. In this tale, the son is killed, but his heart was saved by Athena, and he was reborn. There are many resurrection stories stemming from the Dionysus legends. Orpheus was a Dionysian disciple, and he traveled with the Argonauts to save them from the Siren's songs that lured sailors to death. He too entered the "Land of the Dead" to get his wife Eurydice.

Every tale depicts some god in charge of all vegetation, but eventually just wine, being reborn and using wine to bring truth to mankind. One legend relates a tale where Dionysus was kidnapped by some Etruscan pirates. They had no idea who they had captured until he conjured an enormous grape vine to quickly grow up the ship's tall mast and then sprout grapes. He freed himself by turning all the pirates into dolphins. This scene was painted on a Greek *kylix*, a wine cup, around 550 B.C., so the tale must have been repeated for centuries before that time.

Crete, during the peak of Minoan culture where art and not armies prevailed, accepted Dionysus over Apollo because he was more supportive to ordinary folks. In a land where even women ruled, a god who offered some fun with equal consideration for all, would quickly rise to prominence. A re-reading of Euripides' play, "The Bacchae," will provide deeper insights into the role of Dionysus. While he was an ancient god, in the play he's viewed as a new god. His purpose is to bring wine to the Greeks. It can destroy the state, and it presents a series of paradoxes stemming from wine. Every other year, in or right after March, a *Dionysia* was held. The festival consumed many amphora of wine, music, dancing, and celebrations honored Dionysus for his gift to mankind. It still continues today without any theology, but with an emphasis on the virtues of well made wine at any Gathering of men and women who are seeking to learn more about every aspect of Dionysus' gift, and improve their lives.

In modern Christianity, John's Gospel, so different from the first three, and written a generation after the others, shows the influence of older Greek concepts, and a completely Hellenized Jesus as an equal with God. The anonymous author of this Gospel ignores the Synoptic tradition because he is trying to reach the Gentiles, and would never have been understood by the Jews of his day. Heraclitus of Ephesus used the word *Logos* as we use the word reason back in 500 B.C., and so does John. The Greeks believed that one could never understand a god nor the force of Yahweh, but to convert people, a history and seemingly logical reasons were needed. John was educated in the Greek tradition, and drew on it for his gospel.

Luke's Greek learning helps explain his gospel difference from Matthew. Luke has angels at the birth of Jesus, while Matthew does not. Matthew has the murdering of baby boys, and a trip to Egypt. Luke has no mass murdering event, and no trip. Matthew has a star, and Eastern philosophers visiting, called the Magi, while Luke has no star, and only lowly shepherds at the birth scene. Luke's Gospel reads more like Greek drama, while Matthew is more political as he is trying to get the Jews to accept Jesus. Discrepancies between the Gospels can be traced back to the writer's Greek or Hebrew educational background, and to the time differences as to when they were written. For modern Christians, it's the larger concept that matters most, and not the details; differences should not alter one's faith. Because wine led the way to civilizations, and civilized societies set up rulers, classes of nobility, and a priesthood who give the masses reasons for their existence, and since religions both ancient and modern use wine symbolically, our thesis would be incomplete without noting how earlier ideas and concepts bled into later ones.

Dionysus-like stories were added to the Gospels as time went on. Paul says only that Jesus was born of a woman without mentioning any miraculous type of birth, and he wrote well before any of the Gospels (Galatians 4:4). Mark makes no mention of a miraculous birth for Jesus. The Dionysus concept of a god as the father, and a human mother are introduced into the story later on. The Last Supper concept has countless other earlier examples where wine represents the blood of life. Seeing the full history of spiritual concepts and beliefs from the Stone Age through the Iron Age, as one continuous picture, simply adjusted for the customs and beliefs of different ages, may, in fact, make modern theology easier to accept and to be more rational for many. Without wine, however, we lose so much of the symbolism behind our history.

One final concept for consideration is the Jewish knowledge of the Greek theater.

Herod the Great was responsible for theatrical productions coming to Jerusalem. His citizens were exposed to the concepts of both Roman and Greek productions. If Matthew was exposed to those concepts, it helps explain the structure of his Gospel. The five elements of drama go back to the time of Aristotle. Sophocles' play "Ajax" provides an example of its organization and similarities to Matthew. *Prologue, Parodos, Episode, Stasimon* and *Exodos* are the five parts for every drama. Because Dionysus was responsible for Drama being a part of life in Athens, and also that Greek tragedy was associated with religious aspects of the time, we're forced to delve into the possibility that Matthew introduced his character as a messianic expectant, followed with the loss of youth, and being forced into adulthood, as when Jesus started his mission, and went to teach at the temple while still so young.

Aristotle's Poetics set rules. He expected there to be Unities of Action, Time, and Place, and Matthew certainly followed them all. Also, the events in his Gospel follow the classic Exposition, then Rising Action, a Climax, which heads into Falling Action, and ending with a Resolution or Dénouement.

It's easy enough to read this Gospel, and place all the events into a section of classic Greek drama. Simply put, the study of wine leads you into an ever-wider horizon of art, literature, theater, and history. Chemistry, biology, and all the other sciences soon followed. The gift of Dionysus certainly was the basis for civilization, and the many different cultures found within them.

*   *   *

All civilizations expand and grow during their initial stages. The wine trade provides the wealth and health to permit its expansion. Succeeding generations, with easy access to riches, and material pleasures, begin a decline of prosperity, and cultural decay. The Greeks, Egypt, Babylonia, and even the extremely early Indo-Aryan societies of India all fell after short or even longer periods of power and wealth. Religions do not do well during eras of prosperity. The promise of heavenly rewards mean more in times of hardship, and all historical religions found themselves weakened during periods of great prosperity and stability.

The theology of the Vedas in India, and later on of Buddha, both evolved long after the Late Stone Age Aryan people emigrated, not invaded, to India after long journeys down from the Caspian shores. Legends say great lights appeared in the sky at Buddha's birth. Miracles of the blind seeing again, the deaf hearing, the lame walking, and even that kings came from afar to see him. Stories like this one tie all the peoples of the earth together in their spiritual legends and theologies.

The early settlers of India knew about wine, but because the more tropical areas are not suited to growing *Vitis vinifera* grapes, they quickly began trading for it. Alexander the Great knew of India's spices, silks, and unique items of trade, as did the much later Marco Polo. India was built on its early trade routes to the west. Wine was carried all over the known earth, and used in every social and religious event. As we trace our modern languages back through Latin and Greek, we find a common heritage even in the Sanskrit of India. We can trace wine's journeys through the same routes that words made, and trace both items back to their earliest sources. Etymological history, tracing the sources of a particular word, goes hand-in-hand with the history of wine.

*   *   *

After Mohammed said that the Angel Gabriel spoke to him, much of the wine-drinking world from Spain eastward to Afghanistan changed. Arabian vintages from Iraq and Syria were consumed every day in Mecca through the late 500's A.D. By 642, just ten years after Mohammed's death, wine was banned in every area that the military of his followers conquered. The great wine producers of Egypt, as well as Spain and Portugal, came under Islamic rule. Mohammed couldn't write so he retold the messages Gabriel supposedly gave him to his disciples to memorize, and at a much later date, his visions were recorded but in no particular order. As with Christianity, the written records came much later than any of the historical events.

Filled with poetry, wisdom, and guidelines for etiquette, hygiene, explanations about Abraham, Moses, Solomon, and even Jesus, the Koran even tells you how to entertain your many wives like Mohammed did with all nine of his. It describes a heavenly paradise as a place where men would receive beautiful women; a place where you could enjoy fruits, and relax eternally to "drink of a pure wine."

It has contradictions like all religious writings do. Early on, it lists the good things Allah gave to people of the earth like water, milk, honey, and "fruits of the vine where you derive intoxicants, and healthy food." Next, it cautions you about gambling and wine saying there is sin in both. While he and his followers were in Medina, a fight broke out between one man from Mecca making fun of another from Medina while they ate, drank, and tried to relax. Mohammed asked God how to keep order, and Allah told him gambling and wine were sinful things that Satan used to destroy mankind. For the rest of Mohammed's life, he ordered 40 lashes from the whip for anyone who was caught drinking wine. Ironically, Mohammed's favorite wife, Ayesha, complained about the new rule and quoted him as saying, "you can drink, but not get drunk." It may have been "drunkenness" and not entirely "wine" that was meant to be forbidden. This forbidden pleasure was included in the magnificent verses of Arabian poetry throughout the 8th century A.D. in the poems of Abū Nuwās, and the world famous Omar Khayyam, in the 11th century, finds his *Rubaiyat* verses filled with positive wine reflections. Other Persian poets like Firdausi in the 900's, Sa'di in the 13th century, and Hafiz during the 14th century all sang the praises of wine.

Records show that Arab doctors, who were clever enough to use tried and true Greek medical knowledge, had the most trouble with the new edict. Much, even most of the medicines used wine to help sanitize and cure ailments. The Sultan Saladin had a Jewish doctor called Maimonides from Córdoba, Spain while it was under Islamic rule. He wrote that the best nourishing food is wine; the food that Muslims forbid.

We all know that there are exceptions to everything, and during these Dark Ages, wealthy ruling Muslims still consumed wine, and permitted its growth and development as long as they could tax it, which they did to extremes. The caliphs, who were both religious and civil rulers, had access to wine. Caliph ruled Baghdad up to 1258, and also in Egypt until the Turkish Ottomans conquered their lands in 1517. That title, used by the sultans, was abolished in 1924. However, back around 850 A.D., Caliph Mutawakkil hosted wine parties that tried to resemble the Promised Land, and the afterlife depicted in the Koran. The Arabs made four designations for the different colors of wine. Persians favored yellow wine while Byzantines liked red. Black and white wines are also noted in their records. In 800 A.D., the poet Abū Nuwās wrote about a Persian paradise called *Khoullar* that was a wine-growing village beside the grape laden city of Shiraz. The Islamic followers lived peacefully with Jews and Christians who enhanced the civilization with tax money from wine sales. Wine from Shiraz supplied Baghdad with caliphs' blessings. As the wine trade declined, so did the prosperity of the area. Centuries later, it is interesting to note, that around 1677 A.D., records talk about glass wine bottles being shipped in cases, and packed in straw for mule transport to the Gulf Coast docks.

Trying to interpret Islam is complex, and so many different groups use only the parts that benefit them. What we know is that by the 13th century, the Turks and Mongols conquered most of the territory that Alexander the Great and won. The Turks were warriors, and less inclined to accept dogma about prohibition until much later when the Ottoman Empire rid itself of so many of the oldest vineyards and wine-making locations.

Spain and Portugal never stopped making wine under Muslim rule, and their societies flourished. Algeria kept its Roman tradition of wine production; Middle Age Europe sought out wines from Cyprus and Crete and even Lebanon where traders from Venice could get it. The Coptic Christians of Egypt still grow vines, and make wine today. Wine was made in Afghanistan, and along the Silk Road, until the last century. As vine growth and wine production declined, wealth faded along with the higher quality of life that civilizations provide. Baghdad with its one and a half million people at its peak, faded to fewer than 60,000 citizens by 1850. The masses turned to hashish as what little wine could be found priced itself out of the general public's range. It should be obvious that as wine disappears civilizations decline.

*   *   *

No other civilization has ever continued as long as Egypt did. They accomplished so much at the sunrise of civilization that it would take volumes to even simply outline it. By the time Amenhotep IV became Pharaoh in 1380 B.C., the priests had control of all of Egypt's wealth. They even had the Pharaohs under their control. They ate, drank, and lived in the best style, not unlike the Popes of the Middle Ages.

Amenhotep noted that even the king's harem at Karnak was working to pleasure the clergy. He saw the sun as the reflecting light of the one true god, and he called him *Aton*.

His monotheism took away the power of the priests. He removed every other god's name from the artwork of the nation, but everything went back to normal as soon as he died. The priests waited their time to regain absolute control. Prior to Amenhotep's time, The "Book of the Dead" scrolls presented the rules that had to be followed. The priests alone performed all the magic. They taught that Isis, the Mother Earth, was sister and wife of Osiris. They celebrated her most in midwinter, late December, when the longer days returned, and all of land's life resurrected. Her temples depicted her nursing her divine child Horus, the god of the sun. She nursed him in a stable, the child she conceived miraculously. Even the earliest of Christians worshiped statues of Isis nursing Horus because it reflected their own story of their Mother of God.

Egypt had hundreds of gods, Anubis, Nut, Nephthys, Ket, and so on, and even each new Pharaoh was a god because he was always a son of Ra, or Amon-Ra, as they said. The divine ruler, and the priests' control of each person's afterlife, made it easy for them to rule, and to live very well. The best wines were always presented to the priests, and by the time Ramses II and III became Pharaohs, even the kings were servants to the priests. For 3,000 years, and countless generations, the Egyptians provided the world with inventions like paper, chariots, and religious legends that the Jews later on modified in their Torah. Even the Roman Elysian Fields had to be gotten to by a ferryman Charon-like character taken from the Egyptians and passed through the Greeks. The Greeks replaced Egyptian gods with their own characters, and all of our gospel stories also have many earlier examples. Thoth, the Egyptian god of Wisdom, was thought to be the author, even in his own handwriting, of the papyrus rolls titled the "Coming Forth from Death by Day". Josiah has a similar tale in his Jewish historical writings.

Every early civilization that saw spring providing a rebirth for the grapevines, and later produced wines from its fruit, wrote about this spiritual gift, and an eternal afterlife with rivers flowing with wine.

Whether the kings and political leaders of these first civilizations wanted the people to consider themselves unique and divine, or possibly they felt that the masses of humanity would obey their dictates if they told them that they came from a god, every set of rulers had its priests to help mandate order. Egypt's Thoth personally gave the Pharaoh laws to be followed. Hammurabi's Code came directly from the Sun-god Shamash. A Greek god gave King Minos the laws for Crete; these laws were given to him by the god on a mountaintop similar to the Moses story. The Persians taught that as Zoroaster prayed on a mountain, Ahura-Mazda visited him as lightning and thunder to hand him the "Book of Law". For wine lovers who seek every detail in knowing wine's history, and the role it plays in the development of civilization, it is very interesting to be aware that the Greeks also called Dionysus the *Lawgiver*. He provided two tablets with his laws for humanity, and like the Moses accounts, they were written on stone.

The stories modern Christians appropriated from the Jews are legends that Hebrew captives picked up from their time in Babylonian captivity. Folklore, from every tribe of people on earth, has an Eden-like paradise tale with special trees growing in it, and many times rivers of flowing wine along with a tale on how humanity lost its immortality by committing some first sin.

It was wine that made all these tribes grow into civilizations, become prosperous, and make scientific, and artistic advances; seeing how each theology is deeply related to one another should bind us all together, and not separate us. Whatever cosmic intellect or energy put all the parts together for mankind to exist is up to each of us to contemplate. Pray or meditate while sipping a glass of wine, and may the Force be always with you.

5

WINES OF THE ROMAN EMPIRE

Traveling Grapes

The Greeks and the earlier Phoenicians are responsible for the grapevine plantings all across southern Italy, but less refined species of grapes also grew there, and further north of Rome, the Etruscans made, and traded a profusion of wine long before the Romans assimilated them. On Sicily, the Greeks built the city of Syracuse around an earlier Mycenaean colony that those earlier Greeks had settled. It took about 250 years for Syracuse to become larger than Athens itself. Wine made everyone prosperous.

As Rome grew and expanded its territory, wine became a major topic of concern; poets like Virgil, Ovid, and Horace wrote prolifically about it. The physician Galen recorded the many uses for wine to better one's health, and even cure the sick. Pliny, the historian, left us the most data on the Roman thirst for wine, and its value as a trade item. However, it is the four masters of agriculture, Cato, Columella, Graecinus, and Varro, who give us the most specific knowledge about their grapes, vineyards, winemaking techniques, and a recorded level about the hierarchy of quality levels found among the Roman wines.

Remus and Romulus, the legendary founders of Rome, may have drunk wolf's mike as infants, but quickly turned to wine as they, and the Empire grew. Rome won the Punic Wars, and then Carthage was defeated over the century or so between 264 B.C. and 146 B.C. Rome defeated Hannibal and his elephants, the Macedonians, and the far eastern Syrians. Because the Roman armies carried wine, which sterilized the drinking water and helped with the digestion of foreign foods, their military usually fought at a full healthy strength against sometimes larger, but sicker, ill warriors. It was wine that helped expand the empire, and broaden their civilization. At home in Rome, wine quickly found a large market, one with many levels of quality in demand for the many levels of Roman society. We know that in 171 B.C., a bakery first opened in Rome. It was needed because the earlier diet of basic porridge and milk was replaced with bread and wine.

Pliny recorded that the Romans had some estates so vast that their owners could never ride around them. It was said that the best lands were reserved for royal villas; next best went to the grapevines, and so on down until only the inferior plots were assigned to basic agriculture. Soils were protected by crop rotation, something we'd forgotten by the 1930's American southwestern Dust Bowls. The Romans planted peaches from Persia, cherries from Pontic Cerasus, plums from Asia Minor, olives and figs from Africa, apricots from Armenia, and of course, grapes from Syria, in places that hadn't already been growing vines that had been put in by earlier societies living in that area. Pliny listed twenty-nine fig varieties, and says that there were thousands of orchards; vineyards, unlike all the other designated farming items, were everywhere! They produced over 50 types of wine, and the city of Rome itself drank twenty-five million gallons, which is 125 million modern-sized bottles a year. That was about two full quarts a week for everyone living there: men, women, and child, or for every free person, and every single slave.

Most of the wineries were government-sponsored facilities making a product the Romans could export. They sold to beer-drinking places that would later be called Germany, France and England. It wasn't until centuries later, when Gaul, and North Africa began to plant their own grapes, that Roman wealth began to falter, and its society showed its first signs of decline.

A writer from Carthage, Mago the First, had recorded all the best rules for agriculture with records taken from the Canaanite, and Phoenician traditions. In 146 B.C., the Romans had all 26 volumes translated into Latin and Greek. They used the best ideas, and advanced quickly without having to make the trial and error mistakes of much earlier decades. Their grain farms, and vineyards, quickly produced an abundance of quality products. It was during this period that "first-growths" of Roman wine were first recorded. The vintage of 121 B.C. would have received at least 95 points in our modern rating systems for wine.

Across Italy, at this time, you could find an inn about every 30 or so miles. It served as a shopping center, a bar and a brothel. The Empire had at least 51,000 miles of stone-paved roads. Italy alone had about 12,000 miles of paved, quality highways. Romans traveled. Seneca tells us that Romans went to remote sites, and Plutarch called his countrymen, "globe-trotters". Romans vacationed in Greece, Asia, and Egypt. They studied the doctors, philosophers, and business leaders everywhere they went. They carried and drank only wine on their journeys staying healthy with no need of the Imodium that we modern travelers all carry. Trading wine led to the expansion of items bought and sold. Rome became a civilization of luxury with material abundance such as the ancient world had never seen, nor could possibly conceive.

Using Mago's format, The Roman, Lucius Columella, provided so much vineyard and winemaking information that his concepts were used through the Middle Ages, and into 15th and 16th centuries throughout all of Europe. Columella provided specifics. He came from Cadiz in Spain and grew up among vines. He wanted vines planted two steps apart down the row, and also between the rows. Vines were to be supported on stakes of Chestnut standing at a man's height, and he even wrote about production levels that had to be limited to what today is considered a quality harvest of about 60 hectoliters per hectare. He said that a full cattle skin called a *culleus* held about 20 amphora, or 500 liters, which comes to 60hl/ha. He wrote about different types of trellising, and even explained why growing vines *arbusta* style, or up a tree, helped make good wine. He explained that the tree roots dry out the soil, and he knew grape vines like dry stony soils. He pointed out that the mid-hill side was perfect, the top, good, and the lower, wetter hillside the least impressive vineyard site. Lucius Columella criticized wealthy people who wanted a vineyard simply for status, but never researched the best soils for specific types of vines. He said they quickly tired of pruning, and produced heavy crops of really bad wine. Little has changed today, especially on America's East Coast.

Columella suggested ideas and how to grow vines for many different locations like lying them on the ground in circles as they do in parts of Greece today; head-pruning styles as the modern French call it *gobelet*, various trellises, and a high pergola as I recently saw being reinstated in Abruzzi and in Marches, Italy for the Montepulciano grape; it's designed to help block the excessive sun from burning the grapes, and also to keep alcohols levels down.

The top vineyard of Rome was *Falernum*, which was on the west coast between Rome and Naples. There was now a market for luxuries, and wine was among the most prestigious of items that were being sought. There was a mystique for foreign items, and foreign wine was still imported even though Rome produced massive volumes of wine right at home. However, one of the best of wines came from the vines the Greeks had left behind in southern Italy; it was always considered the best. The ancient *Amineum* vine produced the grapes that made *Falernian*, the top "First-growth" during this period. *Balisca* and B*iturica* vines, Columella says, can also produce top quality wines. The *Nomentan* grape was considered second best to the others. The *Arcelaca* grape may be the great-grandparent of the modern Riesling. All of the highest rated wines were white and sweet, and came from south of Rome all the way down to Pompeii. It wasn't until near the decline of the Roman Empire that tastes changed from wanting thick sweet white wines toward light fruitier reds, that the most prized vintage selections came from up the Rhone River, and toward the Atlantic coastal area of today's Bordeaux.

During the reign of Augustan, 27 B.C. to 14 A.D., the top wines were heated like Madeira is today, and mixed with water, even seawater, so they must have started out very strong with high alcohol levels. Roman writers at the time of Pliny recorded that the Pompcii area produced three types of wine: *austerum, dulce,* and *tenue,* or dry, sweet, and light-bodied. The top rated *Falernum* must have been quite strong even though wine can only get to 15 or possibly 16 percent alcohol by natural fermentation. In any case, Pliny said that *Falernum* ignited when it was near an open flame! *Caecuban* was ranked in second place, and sometimes was equal to *Falernian* even though it came from a wet wooded area.

Pliny rated, very highly, a wine grown where the Pope now resides around Saint Peter's Square. His fourth "Grand cru" was *Surrentinum* produced in Sorrento south of Naples. It was lighter-bodied, and made from the *Amineum* grape. It's said it took 15 to 20 years to mature, and develop the aromas and flavors that the Emperor and Senators would enjoy. Pliny listed *Mamertine* from Sicily, *Hadrianum* produced on the Adriatic coast, and *Rhaetic* wine, made near today's Verona, among the best and his top wines. His complete list is easily researched, but it's important to comprehend that while Rome made and sold great wines in the style of the day, it also continued to consume Greek styled wines grown in Greece's old colonies.

The Romans produced wine made from grapes grown in nearly every province of today's Italy except Tuscany, which was a thickly wooded area, and would take too much labor and expense to clear for vineyards.

The growth of wine production, and its consumption coincides with the growth of Rome's civilization. It was the drink of both the nobility and the peasant. Before Vesuvius destroyed Pompeii, there were about 200 taverns in the city. Some short hundred-meter streets had as many as eight wine shops on it. Wine was sold in a *cuculella,* or a wine carafe, and except for the top best known growths, it was cheap.

As we've stated, wine was made, stored, and shipped in amphora so the subtle differences, as well as a stamp near the handles, tell us how much was made, and who made and shipped it. From these relics, we've learned that most of the 62 A.D. harvest was destroyed in a serious earthquake all around Pompeii, and some later wines were forgeries of that vintage. The same thing happened in every century. A few wine merchants from Pompeii were so famous in their day that we've found amphora with forged stamps using their names. The fake wines sold in the late 20th Century A.D. are nothing new in the timeless world of wine, and the civilizations it built.

The top importer-exporter at Pompeii was Marcus Porcius. He and his family became very wealthy trading wine over three generations. His was not from a noble family, but a carved record at Apollo's temple says he was the major factor in building the city's theater, as well as its amphitheater. Wine tends to buy respect, as well as envy, and wine was a major source of wealth in all of these early Iron Age, and late Bronze Age civilizations.

The massive eruption of Vesuvius in 79 A.D. is estimated to be at least ten times bigger than the 1980 eruption of Mount Saint Helens. It destroyed Pompeii, and also the next nearest city, Herculaneum. The ash, however, did preserve the artwork, and the recorded history of Roman viticulture. We know that Romans made their wines in clay-based *dolia,* similar to the Greek *pithoi,* which were close to the earlier Georgian *kwevri.* All were set into the cool ground. The records of amphora tell us how much was made and shipped with remarkable detail up to just past 250 A.D. From that time onward, it's very difficult to figure out the volumes of wine, their sources, and their destinations. The archaeological wine-related artwork shows wooden barrels being used from that time onward, and wood does not last through the ages like pottery does.

Between 96 A.D. and 180 A.D., Rome had rulers who built, set up social programs, and showed the gods that mankind had left its caves, vacated its wooden villages, built grand cities and civilizations, where luxuries led to restful times, and wine could be savored and enjoyed. The studies of Emperors Trajan and Hadrian alone, could fill volumes about what and how the Romans evaluated their civilization, but for our current purposes, all we need to be aware of is that grape growing, and winemaking flourished bigger and better than ever before.

The Roman writers, poets, playwrights, and historians all recorded the merits of wine, and they tell how every level of society used it. Horace, when thinking about his own impending death, went so far as to write he'd miss his wife almost as much as he'll miss his wine cellar, and its magnificent old wines.

In Avellino, in Campania, the Mastroberardino family presently makes wines that may be traced back to the Romans. Pliny described a vine with white runners that are divided into two sections just as today's Greco di Tufo is. The Greco grape, and the red Aglianico grape, early on written as *Ellenico*, both mean the "Greek" grape. The Aglianico is at the heart of the modern local red wine called Taurasi, and both of these grapes may have made what the wealthiest Romans consumed near the end of the Roman Empire. Mastroberardino also makes a Fiano; it's a unique white wine from early Roman sources, not Greek. Fiano is the grape thought to be the grape Pliny called *appianum*. The wine is dry, balanced, and delightful with opening seafood or vegetable courses. Still growing on Vesuvius is Pliny's *Piedirosso* or "red-stemmed vine" that we know today as Lacryma Christi. It's often consumed at Easter because the name means "the tears of Christ".

With the decline of the well-ordered Roman Empire, all of Europe, North Africa, and parts of the Middle East fell into what we now call the Dark Ages. They lasted until one of the greatest vintner-kings of all time, Charlemagne, united much of Europe, rebuilt the wine trade that is the basis of civilization, and provided a political light that began to shine and brighten the start of the Middle Ages that were to follow in just a few hundred years. We'll have more to discuss about Charlemagne later on.

6

GAUL DURING THE DARK AGES

Early European Vineyards to Charlemagne

In the early 3rd century A.D., wine shipments from the fading Roman Regions began to be transported in wooden barrels instead of baked clay amphora. Without fragments of ancient clay amphora, it becomes quite difficult to confirm records of volume, or who made the wine, or where it was from. The barrel, that we're familiar with, was invented by the Celts. While deserts and treeless plains provided an unlimited clay supply, central and northern Europe was covered with trees so wooden products were numerous. Wood and even metal became the invaluable items for the Celtic races. It seems that with the arrival of wine, there came advancements in technologies; iron tools from the 5th Century B.C. have been found in Europe. The later Romans used wooden stems to encircle barrels, but the Celts made barrels with iron hoops.

Wine in wood, because it breathes, cannot be laid away to age as long as wines stored in amphora can age. However, for shipping, wine barrels are superior, and today they are used and even designed in the same shape that they were made during the Dark Ages.

Were there *vignerons* in Gaul, the ancient Europe, during the Stone Age, or early Bronze Age? Some Frenchmen like to think it was their early ancestors who invented wine, but I think not. The

Greeks, Persians, and the Etruscans all shipped wine up Gaul's rivers, and during later periods of the Roman Empire, as their legions held territory further north, they planted vineyards for the troops to have wine to drink, and made additional wine to trade. When those northern tribes arrived in Gaul, there were no vines planted along the northern Mediterranean coast let alone in the colder European northern areas. The 5th century B.C., in Gaul, was void of vineyards, also void of formal society's advancement. It was without wine, and therefore without any structure of civilization.

The Greeks developed the colony at Marseilles in 600 B.C. Later on, the Romans took it over, and expanded it in 125 B.C. when they increased the trading of wine with the Celts throughout what is now France, Germany, and even Great Britain. Then, just as the early Gauls were maturing from total barbarism, they ran into Julius Caesar, the newest Roman general in the 1st century B.C. Caesar brought order, and commerce to Roman Europe. It's said that by the time he advanced up to the Loire Valley at Chalon-sur-Saône, he found merchants from Rome there who were already selling wine. They used the rivers to carry wine up into Europe, and then began to plant local vineyards from the German city of Trier, to the Atlantic Coast city of Bordeaux; vines were starting to be grown wherever people became civilized. The 4th century Roman poet Ausonius planted his vineyard in what is now Saint Emilion, and today Chateau Ausone is ranked along with Chateau Cheval Blanc as the top two wines from that region. Of course, wild vines grew all across the continent, but the locals didn't know how to domesticate them as their earlier ancestors from Georgia, and all around the Black Sea, had done thousands of years earlier.

Pliny wrote about the *Allobrogica* grape, the same grape that the poet Virgil had praised. It was planted along the Rhone River, and grape scholars think it is what we call today, Petite Syrah, or the Durif grape. Some see this grape as the ancestor of the Pinot family of grapes that are grown today throughout the world: Pinot Grigio, or Pinot Gris as it's called in France, Pinot Blanc, and Pinot Noir may have descended from *Allobrogica*. Oenological research shows that the *Rhaetic* grape may well have become northern Italy's Refosco grape, and the Roman *Mondeuse* grape is, or at least is related to, the Syrah of the modern Rhone Valley.

As the Persians attacked the Roman East, the barbarians took the opportunity to rebel. The Roman edict to stop selling them wine forced the Germans and Franks into full rebellion. Wine consumption, and the wine trade, died at the same time. As the Roman Empire fell to the Franks, Goths, Vandals, and Visigoths, Europe entered the Dark Ages as Attila and his Huns ravished the remains of a civilization that wine had built. Only the new Christian Church remained in Europe, and it was organized on the Roman political structure. The biggest positive event the newly founded Christian Church experienced took place in 496 A.D. when Clovis, a Frankish pagan ruler, was baptized. That reopened a door to plant vineyards to make wine that was needed for Mass.

Most of the Church's bishops at this time were associated with the wine-producing communes the Romans left behind. This Age may have been dark, but it was not dry.

The Dark Ages could have been a total black out for civilized mankind. It might possibly have pushed the people back into early Stone Age hunter-gatherers had it not been for one man, Charlemagne. A good reason for calling this early post-Christ era the Dark Ages is because historians know so little about it. There are few written records. People now made things from wood instead of pottery, and wood rotted away with time. There are two names for this time period. The two terms overlap, and many scholars call 500 A.D. to the late 1400's simply the Medieval Period. Wine scholars tend to call 350 to about 800 A.D. the Dark Ages, and from 800 A.D. to 1450 A.D., the Middle Ages. The good news was that during Charlemagne's time, the demand for wine began to grow faster, and that helped trade and commerce that provided the wealth that would be needed for the new Age of Discovery, or better known as the Renaissance. However, let's not jump ahead too soon.

During the 5th and 6th centuries A.D., only Ireland still had a strong Church. On the main continent, only the monasteries remained as places of prayer, cleanliness, and viticulture. They needed wine for their Mass, and what they didn't drink they could sell or trade. During this period, Islamic armies attacked Italy and France. They conquered Spain, and moved north all the way to the

Loire before Charles Martel stopped the advance. Martel's son was Pepin the Short, who united a Christian kingdom in and around Germany. Pepin's son was Charlemagne who built the kingdom into an area from Holland to the Pyrenees, and from the Atlantic to the Rheingau region in Germany. Blessed by the Pope, he became the Holy Roman Emperor, and he saved Europe from the Arabs. Maybe even more important, he replanted grapes, improved the quality of wine, and helped expand trade. Some prosperity began to return and got the people ready for a rejuvenation of civilization during the later Middle Ages.

Increased wine production in the French and German areas of Europe kick-started the social revival. It wasn't until the mid-1330's that the famous Clos de Vougeot had its wall built around the entire vineyard, but vines were growing there for centuries before then so that the Cistercian Order of monks could make their wine. The workday was long, and a lifetime was short. It's said 28 years was all that could be expected when you labored in Abby vineyards. Most of the wines that we know of today as the top Burgundy selections came from the vineyards the monks planted at that time.

Benedictines planted a grape called *Beaunois* in Chablis; it's now thought to be the Chardonnay grape. As they received more land as gifts, many times from Crusaders who either bought indulgences, or provided gifts to monasteries to protect their souls before they marched off to fight in the Holy Land, the Orders grew richer. From 1096 through 1290, vineyards planted in and around the small villages like Corton, Beaume, Volnay, Pommard, Nuits, and Vosne, gave birth to great wine. This vineyard expansion also aided the makings of a ranking system for the vineyards sites that even today are listed in the *Appellation Controlée* laws of the French wine industry.

During this period of mass plantings in the church vineyards, the *Beurot* grape was planted. Now, it's called Pinot Gris. The red Burgundy, so loved by the nobility, was made from *Noirien* grapes. The name coming from the word for "night or black", and later, because of its pinecone shape clusters, it began to be called *Pineau* in 1375. That's when the name of this grape was first written down. There's no doubt it is today's Pinot Noir grape. A mutation of *Pineau* was found in the village of Gamay, at the same time that the plague of the Black Death seemed to come to an end about 1365. They thought it was heaven sent because it produced three to four times more fruit than the regular *Pineau* grape, and its vines needed to be grown along a trellis for support. However, because it did not make wine of the same character, weight, strength, nor elegance, as did the *Pineau* grape, it was banned from the established Burgundy villages by the Duke of Burgundy. Sixty years later, his grandson, Philippe the Good continued enforcing the law opposing Gamay in northern Burgundy. He wrote that they had the best wines in all of Christianity, and he would insist that they keep their excellent reputation.

Only with an orderly civilization could regulations like Philippe the Good's be enacted, and have wine's role expand once again as the catalyst for a rebuilt orderly society.

Charlemagne had never learned to write so his secretary-biographer, called Einhard, recorded and provided what he said. The Holy Roman Emperor set strict laws about winemaking hygiene, even to the point of preventing foot-stomping grapes. This helped improve the concept of the wine press that early Romans first used. However, cumbersome wine presses were very expensive, and only vineyards owned by nobility or the Church could afford them. Foot crushing continued throughout the Middle Ages, and continues today in a few places in southern and Eastern Europe. Charlemagne also stopped the use of animal skins for storing wine. There were few people who remembered how to properly cultivate vines since so much knowledge was lost during the Dark Ages, but the monks still did. It wouldn't be for another six centuries that the greatest winemaking improvements would take hold. In 1487, the German authorities gave permission to add sulphur to the grape must. It killed bad microbes, and slowed oxygen from darkening and turning the wine to vinegar so quickly. The white, lower alcohol German wines, needed something extra to help preserve them, and somehow they stumbled onto what is now common practice everywhere, and for nearly every wine. Their use of sulphur continues today as the best possible preservative to keep wine fresh and from fading in color.

Charlemagne gave the churches the right to tax, or take a tenth part of, called a *tithe*, what the peasants made, so the monasteries increased wealth because of the extra volume they had to sell. New wealth increased the church's farmland, which usually included many of the vineyards.

A legend states that while boating up the Rhine, Charlemagne noticed that the snow had melted on the south side of a high hill near Johannesburg, so he ordered that grapevines be planted there. Vineyards still grow in the locations he recommended. He did the same in Burgundy at a slope in Corton. He gave the location to the Abbey of Saulieu in the year 775, and the white wine bottled there today is called Corton-Charlemagne. His insight for vineyard locations was excellent, and the wine grown and produced at Corton-Charlemagne is always ranked among the best Burgundy of each vintage even in today's market.

Monasteries sprung up everywhere. The Holy Roman Church got very rich, and trade expanded even though moving wines was not easy. Britain drank more wine from Germany than from France. Vikings raiders struck all the way down to Bordeaux. In 863, monks from St. Martin at Tours won a land grant from King Charles the Bold for a vineyard site at Chablis. In 1000 A.D., Paris was just a village, but the area was already becoming the focal point for religious and commercial projects. While this was happening, Leif Eriksson became the first European to visit North America. He landed, it is suspected, on or near Cape Cod, and called the place *Vinland* because of all the wild grapes growing everywhere. Because he made at least two trips to North America, I'd suspect that his men might have fermented the first American wine at his settlement. A discovery in 1960 of a Viking settlement in Newfoundland confirms Eriksson's achievement. Before he died around 1020 A.D., King Olaf commissioned his followers to spread Christianity around Greenland, and you can't have Christianity without wine. Good wine can't be made there so it had to be bought. Once again, wine became the item that fostered more trade that brought wealth, which in turn expanded societies to broaden and rebuild a civilization.

For the two hundred years after the Viking plundering ended, and their descendants settled in northern France as Normans, trade and wealth accelerated across Europe. As the Roman agricultural writer Columella recorded, vineyards need vast investments, and so it seems money became available to expand wine production. The population grew as wars ceased and cities developed. Without the slave system of the Romans, the Royal families who owned the land got poor locals to plant, grow, harvest, and make their wine. The poor *prendeur,* as the locals were called, owned the vines, but the *bailleur,* the royals, controlled the land. The skills the monks had kept alive spread, and wine once again was the key agent into an expansion of civilization, at least in Christian Europe.

Wine was quite thin and mostly colorless during the Dark Ages, and it wasn't until the post-Charlemagne era, when wine presses were improved, that many wines gained more depth of color. Recall that the Romans first used a screw press in the 2nd Century A.D., but only in the Middle Ages did the complete basket press become the universal way to make wine. This press increased the volume by nearly 20% over foot treading. More color pigments were also extracted from the skins making darker, richer wines. It also pressed in more tannin, and young wines were more bitter; pressed wines set a pattern for aging so that big, full-bodied wines had time to soften them. The additional complexities that evolved in the aged wine with time were an unexpected additional reward. The value of aged wines was also something that was forgotten after the fall of Rome. Good wine demanded that technology be advanced as civilization, once again, began to flourish.

When Pope Clement V set up a rival papacy at his new chateau in Avignon, the wine we drink today, Châteauneuf-du-Pape and the entire Rhone region, once planted by the Roman Empire, began to blossom again. Wine flowed more smoothly than did the politics of the Church, and wine kept on a straight path heading forward.

The *Liber de Vinis* is the earliest wine book ever published. It was written by Arnaldus de Villanova, a doctor who taught at Montpellier University. Sadly, he drowned in 1311 A.D. The book taught the process of racking wine, or moving it off the dead lees into a clean barrel to age, what additives to use much as Pliny had done for the Romans, and even that tasting in the morning gave more honest results when ranking the qualities of different wines. Even today, most wine competitions begin early in the morning to select the best, or at least narrow down the field. We have tasting notes from Geoffrey of Waterford who rated *Vernache* wine, today the Vernaccia from Umbria in Italy, as better than the higher alcohol Greek examples. Very few wines were able to age, so they had to be drunk during the year following their harvest. Even then, the majority of even slightly aged wines were *maderized*, or oxidized, heading toward vinegar. Notes can be found that praised the sensational vintage of 1396 for Chablis, and it's recorded that this wine lasted a remarkable four years. I've aged modern Chablis for over a decade, even two, and found this modern white Burgundy still capable of granting old Chardonnay drinkers the complexities that wine lovers during the Middle Ages strove to obtain.

Lo Crestia, or The Christian, written in the 14th Century, by Francesc Eiximenis, was about morals. In the section on gluttony, he records rules and restrictions on wine drinking. He writes about *Tribi*à wine, which is most likely today's Italian Trebbiano. He praises the Italians for all drinking from their own cup while most Europeans shared only one cup that they passed around. Remember, the Italians also invented the fork, and Florence is where the Renaissance began. Eiximenis was born in Spain, educated at Oxford, and died in France in 1409. He promoted good manners, and without manners, a civilization quickly degenerates taking quality wine with it.

How important was wine during these darkened ages? During the 6th Century, a civil law of these early Franks had at least twice the money on the head of a winegrower than on a farmer or shepherd if an accidental death occurred. The French and German wine towns of today date from the years 800 to 1200, when vineyards were so abundant, that it was said that if the Rhine couldn't ship its extra wine to France, the people of Alsace would drown in it. Many Alsatian wine producers today trace their winemaking families back to the end of the Middle Ages. Many places along the Rhine today are completely planted with vines, and have been since 1226. There's not a tree left to remove or a spot remaining to fit in a vine it was said. It's recorded that by the year 1400, just over 100 million liters of wine a year were shipped through Strasbourg to the rest of Germany, Switzerland, and England. Production, and of course consumption, rose to levels unthought-of as the Italian Renaissance was starting, and civilized ideas of reason, art, and social concerns, once again began to flourish. Sadly, it would all come crumbling down with England, Spain, and the Holy Roman Empire Thirty Years War from 1618-1648. Wine was not to blame. Wine, however, may have been the only commodity that helped end that multi-decade long tragedy.

7

CIVILIZATION FALTERS IN THE MIDDLE AGES

Wine Brought Light to End the Dark Ages

Nearly a quarter century before Shakespeare was born, the amazing vintage of 1540 produced an extraordinarily sweet Steinwein. Back in 1961, a surviving bottle was opened in London; the 421-year-old wine, according to its tasters, was still wine. It looked and tasted almost like a Madeira. Of course, as the air hit it, the wine quickly faded into a vinegary liquid. This was a wine from the beginning of the Age of Enlightenment when viticulture had started to become a basic science, and ignorance began to fade as scientific knowledge begot wisdom. Human culture was rebounding.

Right after the Dark Ages, and at the termination of the Middle Ages, Europe once again had its ups and downs, with senseless wars, plagues, and excessive religious control that was not unlike the power the Egyptian priests had over the Pharaohs. The famous 1540 vintage proved that with excellent weather, and knowledgeable winemaking, this catalyst to civilization was a symbol, yes, even the focal point of mankind living better. The Dark Ages had lost so much of the knowledge that earlier times had worked so hard to learn that Roman and Greek wisdom had to be rediscovered.

The Holy Emperor Charlemagne was the catalyst that helped bring the Dark Ages to an end. He planted vineyards. He established strict rules about being hygienic with regards to winemaking. He encouraged every village to establish vineyards from Burgundy through Germany. From Champagne, to the Rhine and Mosel, the profits from wine began to be seen in new buildings, bridges being built, and a partnership between merchants and local farmers, along with church officials, to bring better social order to the towns and small cities. By the end of the Crusades, Europe was looking forward to growth in trade between wine and textiles. England developed a vast thirst for wine. In 1307, King Edward ordered 1,000 tonneaux of claret just to drink at his wedding. By the end of the Hundred Year's War in 1453, Burgundy was ready to compete with Bordeaux; if not in volume, at least in quality.

*   *   *

During these Middle Ages, Bordeaux and much of France were controlled as part of England. Ausonius planted his vineyard there when it was an active Roman outpost. Today Chateau Ausone, along with Chateau Cheval Blanc, are the premier Grand Cru First Growths of Saint-Emilion. The region has always had uncivilized invaders come to settle there. In 414, the Visigoths pushed out the Vandals who had arrived in 408, and also the Goths who came in 406. None of these societies planted grapes, and they all failed, but by the time the English King Henry Plantagenet had control, the British were looking for more wine; trading then expanded, and the populations grew.

The wine fleets during this Middle Age period were called co*gs* because they were rounded ships. Capacity was counted by the volume of *tuns,* or wine barrels, which they could carry. The sale of wine, and the taxes imposed upon these wine shipments, provided both the French and the British a large part of their economic existence.

The French word *tonneau* is the English *tun,* or the modern word ton. It held 252 gallons of wine. Its size made it too difficult to work with, so for loading on ships, it was diverted into two *pipes,* or four *hogsheads*, which are today called *barriques*, with each barrique holding 225 liters; the volume of our modern barrel.

The regions, and the city-states of France, as well as most of Europe could now grow quality wine, and even more important, they were able to ship it by river to a coastal port. Slower prosperity grew in places like Burgundy, where they had to move their wines over land routes. They had a much harder time selling their wines because land shipping was much more expensive than the cost of barge delivery. *Froissart's Chronicle*, dated 1372, records seeing 200 cargo vessels at the entrance of the Gironde at Bordeaux. Neither the Black Death, nor the Hundred Years War, could stifle wine's increasing importance during the Middle Ages. However, shipping cost rose to 22 shillings a ton. It was only eight shillings a ton prior to the wars, but all progress cost money.

The religious political activity just before and during this time period included a priest named Bertrand de Goth who took advantage of the need for more wine. He planted his Pessac property near Bordeaux with recorded terraced vineyards. In the year 1300, just over 900 ships sailed from Bordeaux with wine for England. De Goth later became Pope Clement V, and set up his new papacy at Avignon instead of in Rome.

In 1453, the Hundred Years War concluded. Joan of Arc's efforts faded as Henry V retook most of northern France. Back in England, the York clan, and the Lancaster's, began their civil war. Burgundy, with Gascony's aid, was able to dislodge the English. The surrender of Bordeaux from the British to the French in 1453 concluded 300 years of England's control over their favorite wine producing area. Bordeaux would be forever more under the control of the French. It was the later wars that forced the English to help develop wines from the Canary Islands, Madeira, Oporto, and the new creations of Sherry from southern Spain. Their desire for this style of stronger, sweeter, wines stems from 1099, the final year of the First Crusade. It was a growing desire for these types of full-bodied sweeter wines that continued the advancement of civilization through the sixteenth, seventeenth, and eighteenth hundreds.

The Holy Land had been under Muslim control for four centuries before the Tartars of Turkey took over the area. Earlier Muslims were respectful of Christian pilgrims, and noted that Jesus was praised in the Koran. The Seljuk Turks studied very little of the Koran, and planned invading further into Christian lands. Right after the First Crusade took back the Holy Land, the only one of all eight Crusades that was successful, monasteries were built, and vineyards were planted there while the same increase in vineyard planting was happening back in Burgundy and Germany. Although it was contrary to their religion, the Muslims knew money would be made from the wines, and they permitted it as they helped make sales, and gathered vast amount of taxes. The same thing happen when the Ottoman Turks took the Greek Island of Santorini in 1579. The conquerors encouraged wine growing, and joyously collected taxes on the wine for themselves. Wine may be the source of all civilizations, and tax money derived from wine may be the source of all political tax developments. Did the politicians who enacted the American Prohibition laws ever study any history at all?

The Moors were never without wine. Their Arab empire spread westward to the Andalucía region of southern Spain. They called it *Al-Andalus*; Andalus meant, "Where the light ends" or the most western sunset. Toledo became Christian in 1085. El Cid, the Christian folk hero, was the Moors' biggest problem. Even though these Muslims took control of Spanish towns, they forced no one to change their religion, or give up their property. They taxed wine, and encouraged its production. In 1236 the Arabs lost Córdoba, then lost Valencia in 1238, and Seville fell in 1247 as the Moors left Europe. By the end of the 1200's, all of Spain had vineyards, and wherever the Cistercian monks set up monasteries, the wine was excellent and costly. This expanded wine trade quickly brought Spain out of the Dark Ages, into the Middle Ages. It also provided funding for their great age of exploration. In 1423, a wine law set of rules was enacted for who, when, and how much wine, could be shipped into their capital.

An interesting side note is about a wine called Tent, which is now extinct. The British called this wine Tent; the Spanish called it *tintilla,* and drank it after their dinners up until about 1830. It was made from grapes that had red, not white juice as all other wine grapes have whether they're red or white grapes. Tent was more like the traditional claret wine. Samuel Pepys, the man who first mentioned Chateau Haut-Brion, had a cask of Tent in his personal wine cellar, and it was printed on menus during the Victorian age.

Monemvasia was the grape that grew very well on the Greek islands, and also in the Holy Land. It was called Malmsey, or Malvasia by Europeans drinkers. Along with the Muscat grape, these two varieties produced the wines the Crusaders valued most. Even though the third Crusade was hardly successful, Richard the Lionhearted took control of Cyprus, a land filled with Muscat, and helped create a wine trade that lasted right into modern times.

As populations grew, and city-states expanded during the late Middle Ages, the city of Venice had become the leading influential city. Venice shipping dominated not only the wine cargo, but she also led the way in types of trading all merchandise. After Venice's decline as an independent shipping region, conflicts between England, Spain, Holland, and France continued. The Dutch dug out, and drained the marshes of Bordeaux, so grapes could be grown on the newly formed dry land. The different French regions competed with each other to gain England as their primary customer. Spain, and even Portugal, made wines to suit their British clients, and they even let the British design the style of wines they wanted. However, it was Venice that extended its colonial territory so it could plant sugarcane, grapevines, and cotton to sell in areas both toward the East and in the West. Where wine was bought, cities grew and civilized endeavors expanded. On the islands and areas where Venetians were in charge, food production declined, and populations had to migrate because the only items permitted to be planted were items the Venetians were selling.

Venice was also famous for its glassmaking. The skill and ability to make fine glass had been lost after the fall of the Roman Empire. By 1300, the nearby island of Murano, was famous everywhere for affordable clear glass that was ideal for enhancing fine wines. It was only after the Turks blockaded Venetian shipping, that Venice encouraged more winemaking inland around Verona and Padua, where today's villages of Bardolino, Valpolicella, and Soave, still produce everyday drinking wines in huge amounts. Prior to the blockade, Venice traded for wine all around the Adriatic looking for Greek-styled strong wines with a touch of sweetness. The cafés of Venice provided *Prošek* made from the *Marastina* grape on the island of Hvar. They had a powerful Čara-*Smokviča*, which must have smelled and tasted like the Glara grape, but was totally unrelated to today's Prosecco. They sold wines made from half-sun-dried grapes in the style of today's Amarone wines. Wines made with the same technique and style were the *Grk* from *Korčula*, and *Postup* and *Dingač* from the peninsula of *Pelješac* in southern Dalmatia, which is in today's Croatia, and also *Vugava* wine from Vis. These sweet Malmsey-style wines were best suited for further trading, and re-export than to sell to the locals of Venice who preferred drier wines. In any case, Venice grew rich from wine, and they built a civilized city-state funded by a wine-trading empire.

When the city-state of Florence opened its port at Pisa, it saw the chance to get ahead of Venice. Noble families like the Frescobaldi, and Antinori clan, invested quickly; the Antinori family went into the wine business in 1380, and anxious Venice quickly imposed a tax on their Florence Malmsey trade. King Henry VII of England quickly imposed an import tax on Venetian ships, which killed the trade for Venetian exporters, and opened the doors for wines from Spain, and Portugal, that the ships from Pisa now carried. Florence got richer as Venice declined proving once again that civilization depended upon wine.

When the Turks captured Cyprus in 1572, the locals were at last permitted to plant what they needed, rather than what Venetians sold. Planting grapes, and making wine, not only created civilizations, it, in a few cases, helped cause the decline of some societies.

The long trade war between Venice and England over shipping the Malmsey that was so desired was what caused Malmsey-style wine to be made in Spain and Portugal. Higher alcoholic, sweeter wines would be the drinking fad until the end of the Middle Ages, and even into the new Age of Enlightenment that followed.

The demand for sweeter, stronger wines continued to grow. Portugal and Spain competed for world trade routes to ship wine, and bring back silver, spices, and gold. It is recorded that Magellan, whose ships made the first trip around the entire world, spent more on sherry than on his weapons and armaments. Interesting. Only 18, of his 237 men, every saw home again. It would have been even fewer if it weren't for the sherry wine they carried with them.

Many new wines were written about during the late Middle Ages. Portugal made a Bastardo, and still does from the eponymous grape. Early wine writers said it was simply a mix of wine and honey, but when Shakespeare, in Henry IV, Part I, has Prince Hal say, "Your brown Bastard is your only drink," the reference is to the Portuguese wine, not some illegitimate homemade drink.

In the 1300's, Chaucer, the first English poet to write in his native language, wrote about wines from Lepe, which is a village in Spain between Algrave and the more famous Jerez. Chaucer writes, about the Lepe in the Middle English of his day, saying, "*of which there riseth such fumositee*", and that having only three drinks of it, he won't even know where he is. Chaucer's father was an importer of Spanish wines, and not a shoemaker as his Old French last name might suggest. At the other extreme, the Portuguese thought their *Ribadavia* wine was their best wine, and wanted it to replace Lepe, but the English found it so acidic they could hardly drink it. It was quite similar to today's Vinho Verde that's made in northern Portugal.

Spain experienced its greatest period during the 1500's. They controlled the oceans, and most of the newly found western world. They promoted civilization. They took grapevines to their new colonies, and made wine to be used as a healthier drink than the local water. Their conquests, they thought, were triumphs for them, but they were not good for the locals. As it turned out, it was not so good for Spain; for example, during the half century after taking control of Mexico, the price of grain doubled, and the cost of wine went up eight times! Records show one fleet heading to the new world carrying just over 150,000 casks of wine from Andalusia, Malaga, Jerez, and Sanlúcar. That amount of exported wine decreased the local volume for sale, and increased the local cost. By 1578, Santiago was being built in Chile, and the Spanish found an ideal new wine growing area, and once again hurt their home country.

I find it extremely interesting that Magellan spent more money on sherry wine for his crew than he spent on weapons for his first-ever journey around the world. Of all the men that sailed off with Magellan, the 18 that returned to Sanlúcar would never have done so without the wine. I repeat this history to remind us that every sailing vessel since the earliest men floated rafts onto the seas, carried wine with them to help prevent illness on their journeys much as the Stone Age explorers must have carried their first wines with them as medicines, or to trade with strangers, or maybe just to help make friends by sharing their Dionysian gift with others.

In 1453, Gutenberg was printing in Mainz, Germany. The 1400's closed with Venice fading from power and wealth. England lost control of Bordeaux to France. Also, in 1453, Leonardo da Vinci was born, and many historians say that's the date when the Renaissance began. The Duke of Medina abolished all export wine taxes in 1517, and Spain bonded with England at the expense of France. King Henry VIII married the Catholic Catherine of Aragón, and trade prospered until he married Anne Boleyn, became a bigamous, was excommunicated in 1534 just one year later, and made the British wine trade suffer for half a century. For half a century, Andalusia was the only port where British ships could come to pick up wine without being burnt.

By 1597, Shakespeare's lovable drinking man, Sir John Falstaff, was singing the praises of sack. Sack was the nickname for sweet Spanish sherry. He drank it everyday except on Good Friday as Shakespeare wrote; "he sold himself to the Devil for a cup of Madeira…" England was back as a wine-buying partner after 1566, when the Duke gave special privileges to their wine merchants looking for Sherry. After the Spanish exterminated the last known member of the race of Cro-Magnons on the Canary Islands in about 1490, they planted vines, and very soon Canary wines became the rage in London. I never think of Cro-Magnon men as being so modern, but when you recall that the time from now, back to the time of Christ, was about the same as the period of Babylon to the Greeks; all of our recorded history, from the Egyptian hieroglyphics, to the Greek and Roman alphabets, is but a blink of the eye with regards to our total evolution from hunter-gatherer, to living in a civilized society. It seems that wine was the liquid roadway to our modern society. Recall Falstaff in, *The Merry Wives of Windsor,* saying, "If I had a thousand sons, the first humane principle I would teach them would be to forswear thin potations, and addict themselves to sack." From Spain they drank the wine from the *Listan* grape, now known, as the Palomino grape with its higher alcohol, and sweetened with Malmsey, Muscatel, and Pedro Ximénez.

Wine made the Dark Ages bearable, and guided the Middle Ages into a revival of prosperity, so civilization could once again flourish just as it has been doing since the Late Stone Ages. Whenever vineyards flourished, so did mankind.

8

THE AGE OF ENLIGHTENMENT

Spreading the Vine and Civilized Society

Shakespeare's last play, *The Tempest*, was written in 1613. It takes place with ship-wreaked characters on a magical island most likely in the New World. European powers were conquering, setting up colonies, and planting grapes wherever they went, not unlike what the ancient Greeks, and the Phoenicians did. The Dutch and Spanish planted *Vitis vinifera* vineyards when they set up colonies in South Africa, and in South America. Once again, permanent settlements had to be built so men could grow and harvest grapes.

In Europe, distillation made many improved advancements. The first place it was seen as a drink instead of a medicine was in Germany. The Dutch shippers, who had become the modern Venice-merchants of the world, made a fortune with Gin. However, Gin quickly developed a very negative image because of the epidemic of drunkenness in London. Even beer was challenging wine as the favorite drink of England. At the same time that beer made consumption advances, chocolate made its appearance. Sugared into a drink first in Madrid, it soon became a favorite drink in Holland and Italy.

In 1637, a Greek student at Oxford, introduced coffee to England. Soon there were dozens of coffee houses in London just as there were in Constantinople. Coffee cost a penny; beer cost more, but was still cheap. Gin cost a bit more than beer, and wine was considered a luxury. The British shippers in Java learned about drinking tea from Chinese merchants. At first, it was as expensive as wine when only the Dutch ships brought it back to England. The cost fell quickly when the English East India Company started importing it. It was a unique period of social experimentation with liquids to savor. In the end, wine returned as the most valued liquid commodity, and it continued to push civilization forward.

The Dutch became very rich as the British experienced an endemic of alcoholism during the second half of the 1600's. Women drank as much as men. Wine, because of its lower alcohol content than hard liquors, and the custom of it ideally being part of a meal, almost faded away as the Dutch introduced narcotics, and liquid stimulants to Europe. By 1650, the Dutch had nearly 10,000 ships, the largest trading flight in all of history. Like Venice before them, they bought and sold the same items. They sold what they found elsewhere while producing very few items at home. Even while at war with Spain, the Dutch never stopped buying wine from them to sell to the more educated.

They arrived in Bordeaux to buy wine, and stayed on as civil engineers to help drain the marshes. The Dutch were experts, even back then, in water management. They created the vast vineyard areas that today we see as the home of one of the greatest wine producing areas in the world. They loved dark stronger wine, and took all the Cahors wines they could get. As they drained the marshes along Bordeaux's rivers, they provided suitable new land for grapes, and they soon found places where the *Botrytis cinerea* or "noble rot" could produce the sweeter wines that England so desired. Just north of Bordeaux in the Charente region, they encouraged the distillation of the thinner wines in and around the village of Cognac. At the start of the 1700's, the London Gazette printed an ad for Old Cognac Brandies. South of Bordeaux, they easily got the villagers to distill their wine into Armagnac. They called it *brandewijn* or "brunt wine". Both Armagnac and Cognac had ample forest, and therefore enough wood to burn to heat their stills. The process decreased the volume of wine down to about one-seventh when made into brandy, and that made shipping even easier for the Dutch.

While the Dutch got the Cognac winegrowers to make a distillate, it was the Londoners who first noticed its quality over other products of distillation. Other products had to be re-boiled a number of times to rid itself of off-smelling aromas, but Cognac needed only two journeys through the still. Cognac is able to retain some of the original wine's flavor and aromas. The English firms of Hine, Delamain, and Martell where soon set up in Cognac, and were quickly followed by Richard Hennessy from Ireland in 1765.

Oliver Cromwell, who was ruling England between kingships, declared war against the Netherlands in 1652. France too, at the same time, decided it wanted a larger merchant fleet. Louis XIV cut the forest of Limousin and Tronçais to build his fleet. The wood from these two forests was used to age the French Brandies then, and even today. Limousin adds the vanillas noted in Cognac, and Tronçais imparts spice flavors. Louis' fleet hurt Cognac and Armagnac production, but for only a short time.

We've already stated that the greatest change to wine came at the end of the Roman period in northern Europe when the finished product began to be shipped in wooden barrels. The next great improvement came with the advancement of the glass bottle, and finding a good enclosure for it. After the demise of the Roman Empire, wine lovers completely forgot how older wines changed, softened out, and become more complex in taste and smell. This improvement, made by the mid-sixteenth century A.D., started a revolution in wine that remains until today. After nearly 2,000 years, we can once again experience the pleasures that aged wines can provide just as Pliny had recorded.

The glassware made in Venice was praised, but Italian bottles were too thin. The British learned that with hotter cold-burning fires, they could make thicker, stronger bottles. That knowledge came just in time because King James I proclaimed that the glass-houses were destroying all of England's forest, and he forbade using any timber to make glass for anything other than lattices. It was Sir Kenelm Digby who used new coal burning furnaces to make cheaper, stronger, green and brown glass, the same colors that are used today, for wine bottles. Once again it was wine that drove civilized invention forward.

The best way to seal these bottles was with ground glass stoppers. Chateau Lafite used them in 1820. It didn't take long to learn that natural cork from the *Quercus suber* evergreen cork oak would keep the air out of the wine. The corkscrew, first called the "bottlescrew" was modeled from the "steel worm" that was used to retrieve musket balls from black powder rifles that misfired. Everything was now in place to encourage the building of wine cellars, and aging the much-improved Bordeaux wines that the British so loved.

Modern society's educational structures stem from the mid 1600's when the sciences began to demand deeper thought than all the previous eras of blind acceptance of politically controlled religions, and their doctrines. Everything from Art to Agriculture had to be studied. The recently chartered "Royal Society" reviewed a treatise called, *A Brief Discourse Concerning the Various Sickness of Wines, and their Respective Remedies, at this Day Commonly Used.* Wine was often a central theme of advanced education. This 'modern" civilized society wanted to know all it could about wine as both a commercial product, and as an item of social focus. During the 17th Century, wine became a symbol of well-mannered, highly educated refinement. Just as when the early hunter-gatherers settled so they could grow vines, harvest grapes, and then make wine, the Age of the Enlightenment saw the populations advance because of wine's key role in social interactions and commerce.

In France, the Sun King, Louis XIV, had statues carved of himself portrayed as Dionysus or Bacchus in his quest for classical greatness. He knew it was wine that had enlightened the ancients. He also made Champagne, in 1647, the most fashionable drink of his court, and shortly after that, he put the lighter red wine, Burgundy, above all the other popular drinks of his day. Wine was held in esteem above tea, coffee, and all the available spirits, but that specific wine, Champagne, because of its sparkling uniqueness, created a separate life style. The Jean François de Troy painting called, "The Oyster Lunch," depicts the thrill of a flying Champagne cork, and the enthusiasm, for this most sought after wine during the Age of Enlightenment.

*   *   *

It was the Dutch, not the English, who first bought the red wines from Oporto during Holland's military conflict with France at the end of the 1600's. They sought out white wines from Lisbon, and from down in Jerez, but found it easier to expand trading with the reds of Oporto.

At the start of the Eighteenth Century, after nearly 250 years of European exploration, the general populations had settled into a familiarity of being governed by kings who proclaimed that their power was God-given, and everyone else existed merely to serve them. The only relief from the drudgery of common life was provided by wine. The merchants of the day grew into an upper class among all the citizens by trading, and wine was one product that was always in demand. The lowest duties were bestowed on any country that was not at war with you, so the popularity of wines, and its demand, depended upon who had the lowest price. England's many wars with France and Spain provided an opportunity for Portugal to make and sell wines suited to the British taste.

Peter Bearsley hiked up the Douro landscape in search of ideal lands to plant grapes, and make a wine that would suit the British market. He found suitable spots, and after 300 years, his company, after nearly 20 name changes, still deals in Douro wines. Today his company is known as Taylor Fladgate, and they make some of the greatest Oporto wines. The Douro was the river-roadway for getting Ports down to Vila Nova de Gaia, located across the river from Oporto, where they were blended, aged, and bottled. During the early 1700's, Oporto was an average-strength red made as a table wine, or food-wine as we now refer to that style. The Douro currently has hydroelectric plants, and dams, but until the mid-1960's, Port was shipped down the river in a *barco*, an open ship with sharp pointed ends having a single sail with one only mast, and a single steering oar at its rear. The shape and function of these boats is nearly exactly the same as the Phoenician ships that 3,000 years earlier brought wine for trade, and vines to plant in Portugal.

As noted earlier in this work, wine's history is closely related to the history of theology, and during the period of the 1650's through the 1700's, Catholics were killing Protestants in France; the opposite was taking place in England where Protestants murdered Catholics; in Spain the Jews were robbed and murdered, and people were burned to death in Italy, all for the sake of God. In India, however, the Moslem conqueror Akbar discarded Islam, took a Muslim, a Buddhist, and a Brahman woman for his three wives. He accepted all religions, and stopped the killing of Hindus. India made a peaceful, prosperous advancement trading wine, along with all its eastern treasures, until the ruling Moslem minority lost its military control. Hindu India once again took control, and it remains so today.

Wherever and whenever wine has flown freely, civilization has advanced. Every specific example is too numerous to include in a limited work like this, but from the Stone Age through the modern eras, civilization has walked hand-in-hand with wine.

Surveying the Age of Enlightened, you see the British in control, and setting the standards for wine's production. Textile production in Portugal was destroyed by the Methuen Treaty, so unemployed weavers turned to laboring in the new wine region of the Upper Douro. Cheap red wine could easily fill the thirsty British market. They had brandy added for strength, and also elderberry juice to deepen the color. It wasn't until after the great earthquake in Lisbon, when the Marques de Pombal rebuilt the city, that the

Portuguese took control of its Port production. They cut out all the elderberry trees; they began to add brandy in the middle of the fermentation instead afterwards, which added strength, and preserved some of the natural sugars, and they formed the Douro Wine Company that kept 10,000 pipes of Port a year for their Brazilian colony where it was bought with South American gold. As the wine improved, so did the economy. By the mid-1700's, Englishman's wine cellars began to fill with the very age-worthy wine from Oporto.

The Methuen Treaty of 1703 also made the Protestant Prince of Transylvania start a war with the Catholic Austrian army controlling Hungry. The French Sun King, Louis XIV, got involved because he saw an opportunity to obtain more coffee, the drink the Turks introduced when the siege of Vienna ended, and he also wanted access to a famous wine that was made specifically for Popes and Kings: Tokay Essence. After the Turks finally left in 1683, Hungary was ripe for vinous expansion.

From the time the Greeks first carried their vines northward, and later on when the Roman Emperor Probus planted vineyards there, Hungary expanded its cities, and built a civilization with wine as its first source of income. As in France and Germany, the early Church played an important role in improving grape growing, and the quality of its wine. The Bronze Age Celts who settled the area, most likely made and drank wine from wild grapes. The Romans made improvements, but it wasn't until the early Middle

Ages, when Italian guests of King Bela of Hungary, brought grape vines with them that eventually could make Tokaji.

From Italy, Furmint grapes, the highly flavored *Hárslevelü,* and Muscat grapes, took to their new home, and are still the basis for the modern sweet dessert wines of Tokaji. The Tokay Essence was the richest, sweetest, and made only from the free-run juice. It was spoon-fed to dying Popes who, many times, lingered on for some time afterward, most likely, from the sugar infusion energy boost. It was sold and exported as Hungarian Tokay Aszú, a wine, and not a medical elixir, that made it so famous.

Tokay, as labeled today, comes from the *Tokaji-Hegyalja* region of Hungary. This wine has nothing in common with the Tokay d'Alsace, a name no longer permitted by EU law. The wine from Alsace was made from Pinot Gris grapes. This grape was also grown in Hungary, and called *Grayfriar* because of its relation with the earlier church vineyards. It is known today in Hungary, as the *Szürkebarat* grape.

Because of the British sweet tooth for wines, Tokay had a ready-made market, and even though that style goes in and out of popularity, it helped provide an income to build a fresh society after the Turk's departure in the 1600's.

*　　*　　*

When Portuguese sailors first landed at the Cape of Good Hope, they saw nothing worthwhile, just sparse land and savages. They carried wine to trade, and they were looking for India and its spices. It wasn't until 1652 that the Dutch East India Company first planned to plant vines to make wine to sell. In 1654 they received cuttings from Germany, but they failed in South Africa's *terroir*. In 1659, plants from the Canary Islands were planted and soon made the first commercial vintage to sell. However, with fewer than 200 citizens living and working there, the company struggled.

After Simon van der Stel, in 1679, founded Constantia, and sold the Steen, as they called Chenin Blanc, did South African wine become a success and with profits made from wine, a newly settled society could build a civilization. A tasting note from 1692 records says that wines from Constantia are showing much higher quality than all previous wines from South Africa. The Steen plants came from the Loire Valley. Spanish Palomino, French Sémillon and Muscat selections were also making headway. It seems that Shiraz and other reds were also doing well at Constantia, but the sweet Constantia, now lost to history, was what made Cape wines so desired and held in such high esteem.

The British easily overtook the Dutch in 1795 and by 1814, all of Europe knew that England had total control of the Cape and all of South Africa. They left the wine growers alone in Stellenbosch, and viewed the new vineyard area as a replacement to their loss of Bordeaux some 350 years earlier. Lord Nelson referred to the area as an "immense tavern." The British lowered the duty on Cape wines to one-third the level they charged for Portuguese wines. Once again taxes and duties set back prosperity in an otherwise stable society.

In 1418 Portuguese sailors accidentally found an island covered with woods; their word for wood is *madeira*. They soon set fires to clear the land, and it's recorded that forest fires burnt for over seven years leaving loads of ash fertilizer and open spots to plant grapes. Madeira would quickly become a place for a final fresh water stop, and to pick up fresh wine for voyages westward to the new world.

The Spanish, having found the Canary Islands years earlier, had already been producing the maximum amount of wine possible. After they killed off all the native peoples who still lived in a late Stone Age atmosphere, Spain produced a style of wine suited to the cold-weather drinkers of Great Britain: sweet with high alcohol. Madeira quickly devised wines that would soon overshadow the Canary wines.

Canary Malmsey in the fifteen and sixteen hundreds, then Madeira Malmsey in the seventeen and eighteen hundreds had no other competition and were both sought out throughout Europe, especially in England, and also in the new colonies of the New World. A tasting note from Shakespeare on Canary wine says, "… it perfumes the blood ere one can say what's this?" He later has his famous drinking character, Sir John Falstaff wash down a capon's leg with a full bottle of Madeira.

The island had no port-docks. Barrels of Madeira called pipes were floated into the sea to get aboard the ships. A "pipe", sometimes called a "hogshead", averaged 550 liters, about 145 gallons of wine. Records in Funchal, Madeira's largest city, show that in December of the year 1697, 11 ships loaded 695 pipes for journeys to America. The demand for Madeira wines made from the Bual, Verdelho, Muscat, and Terrantez grapes where in fashion and once the producers learned that these wines greatly improved with the rolling of the ocean, the British demanded that their allocation be shipped across the Atlantic and then back to England. By the end of the 1700's, the British ordered Madeira that had to first be shipped around the Cape of Good Hope and on to Bombay, India before returning back to London. Madeira seems to be a wine that has achieved immortality.

Once the Madeira makers figured out that it was the heat at the equator that enhanced the complexity of their wine, they built their first *estufa* in 1794. It was a facility with a heater and pump system to circulate hot water around the wine casks. They eliminated the stench of bilge-water, and improved Madeira to the quality we have today.

Why, it's often asked, did America fall in love with Madeira? Well, the colonies drank what they could get. After Portugal went to war with Spain in the 1640's, Madeira could not get enough food and the American Plantations had an abundance of grain. Savannah, Georgia is located on the same latitude as Funchal. Their

"Madeira Club" still savors century-old bottles; they consumed an 1838 Malmsey, at 150-years-old in 1988, and said that it was almost ready. I savored an 1863 Bual recently and at 155 years old, I agree with my Savannah friends; the Bual Madeira was almost at peak.

Men consuming vast amounts of Madeira wrote the Constitution and Declaration of Independence of the United States. Once again, it was wine that helped forge a new and progressive civilization.

In our day however, England, as well as the Americas, seeks out more Oporto and even more Sherries than they do Madeira. Scandinavian countries now get most of the best Madeira.

*　　*　　*

The newest winemaking techniques stabilized during the mid-1700's. Bordeaux and Burgundy made extensive progress. The Marquis de Ségur controlled, and owned, Chateau Lafite, Chateau Latour, Chateau Mouton, which would become a First Growth Grand Cru Bordeaux in 1973, as well as Chateau Calon-Ségur. With the help of his political friends, Ségur made his wine empire the most profitable commodity at the time. His descendants owned Chateau Latour until 1963. It was "location", just as in Burgundy, that determined the worth of different wines. The Scottish economist who wrote, The Wealth of Nations in 1776, recorded that vines, unlike fruit trees, are affected the most by different soils. "This flavor, real or imaginary, is sometimes peculiar to the produce of a few vineyards…" Adam Smith was correct.

Fr. Bellet, a priest at Cadillac in 1796, listed 20 different white grapes growing in Bordeaux along with 18 red grapes. Because the church was the best organizer at that time, they selected the best grapes to grow in Burgundy, but they held little or no land in Bordeaux, so it would take another century to confirm the best grapes for making both white and red Bordeaux. Wine certainly brings civilization, laws, and order to mankind's societies, but sometimes it takes advanced human thought to set the standards needed for a society, an empire, or even a vineyard to show its best. The Comte de Lur Saluces of Chateau Yquem, the most famous Sauternes, wrote that all the white wines made during the 1700's were sweet. That confirms the British desire for full-bodied, sweet wines that could hold up to shipping, age a bit, and still be enjoyable to a wine-thirsty Great Britain, and all of its colonies.

Burgundy, on the other hand, had already classified its Grand Cru, Premiers, and Village wines, because the Church, which owned most of the great vineyards, kept meticulous records on the growing conditions as well as the wine's final quality. It wasn't until after Napoleon, early in the next century, that Burgundy's great vineyards were broken up into such small sections that the wines, today, depend entirely on who the producer is, and much less the location name. Clos Vougeot, as an example, was one complete Grand Cru vineyard making a great wine; today, it has over 80 owners with some people owning just one or two rows of vines. "Know the producer", and "buyer beware" is what's necessary when it comes to buying famous Burgundies in the modern world. Napoleon brought an end to Church control of Europe's greatest vineyards.

In French-controlled Germany, Schloss Johannisberg, and Kloster Eberbach, were lost forever from their respective Catholic Orders of the Benedictines and the Cistercians; they are two of the greatest German vineyards. Many societies were faltering once again, and so was the world of wine. But, as viticulture and winemaking bounced back, and grew, so did the social order of an expanded Western civilization. Back in 1672, when so many of the German wines were still red, St. Clara's Abby instructed that all the vines should be replaced with Riesling. The Church led the way until Napoleon ended their control. Just as the growers of Burgundy knew Pinot Noir did better in the north, and Gamay was suited best to the south, most of Germany re-planted with Riesling except in Franconia, where its thick, heavy soils with lime, were better suited to the Austrian grape, Sylvaner.

Wine has been a staple with religions since early mankind first set up theological orders and rites; wine added the necessary mystery to religions, and hand-in-hand, wine use in religion helped build so many civilizations over the centuries.

However, prior to Napoleon, during the Age of Enlightenment, available 18th Century vineyard records show that Germany rebuilt, and grew during the same time period that they replanted the country with mostly Riesling. This grape provided the sweetness so desired throughout Europe. Two important things happened during that time. Weather conditions greatly improved during the 1700's, helping Riesling-based wines to improve, and the German Doctor, Eberhard Gockel, found out that the addition of lead to wine, which was done since Pliny advocated its use for excessively tart vintages during the Roman days, was deadly poisonous. Some go so far as to say it was the use of lead that brought down the Roman Empire. Germany avoided that mistake. Constant watch has to be kept for societies to progress positively. During the late 20th century, Austrian wine makers added the glycol of anti-freeze as they tried to sweeten their wines. Thankfully, that practice was discovered, and it no longer happens. Modern Austrian wines are among many of the best wines made in modern Europe.

There are reports from 1762, that wines were adulterated because of demand, and because of high excise taxes. Some Porto was really fermented from turnip juice. There were fake red wines made of blackberries, raspberries, aloes, and turnips. Prior to Gockel's lead poison awareness, lead oxide was added to sweeten the fake wines. Raisin-soaked white wine was sold as cheap Madeira. Scholars of the day, like Henry Fielding, Tobias Smollett, John Locke, and even Thomas Jefferson, all recorded what the actual wines from many European destinations should taste like. Populations who were educated and could read, avoided the rotgut that was sold to the lower classes during this stage of European advancement much like it was done during every age of civilized advancement.

Social order and societies progressed parallel to wine's improvement, and both society and wine made advancements during this Age. Not until the second half of the Twentieth Century, did wine use so rapidly expand, and become a refined commodity of trade in the modern civilized world. The gift of Dionysus had traveled through time with positive consequences, as did much of the civilized world.

9

WINE IN CONTEMPORARY CENTURIES

The 18th through the 21st Century Civilizations

It was wine; its taste, its effects, its health benefits, its trading power, and its ability to adapt and improve that brought mankind out of the caves, and into tiny clusters of dwellings that became villages that grew into cities, then empires. It was wine that was drunk with bread that developed agriculture. It was wine that provided the wealth from trade that funded the building of cities and empires. It was wine that drew vast populations, filled with superstitions, to accept supernatural beliefs. It was wine that caused civilization.

The 19th and 20th Centuries were but a blink of the eye with regards to the centuries since our species survived the last Ice Age, and so will the current 21st Century fly by. It was wine that aided civilized progression over the past 225 years as grapes were planted in every corner of the world.

Napoleon was in Jerez, Spain in 1812. The British were supporting Spain, and busy there until they attacked their former colony, the United States. The French then invaded Russia. Wine quality dropped, and oranges made more profit than fermented grape juice. Late in the 1830's, wine sales improved; they were led by Sherry wines from Jerez. Lord Byron wrote about wine.

Thomas Peacock, the novelist wrote about wine. The British, all the way back to Chaucer, whose father was a Spanish wine importer, seemed to keep their civilization afloat on wine. Wars come and go, but wine never lost its favor among the British people. Five hundred years after Chaucer, John Ruskin, in the Victorian period, reviewed wine and art. Just twenty-three years into the Victorian age, England was drinking more Sherry than Porto, and sales of that wine funded the cost of rebuilding Europe after so much revolution.

The French sold most of their sweet Champagne to Russia, but when they later made it drier, England began to seek it out. The still wines from the Reims area were called Sillery and the last bottle made in that style was in 1814, even though the name Sillery was used until 1900 for white wines from north central France.

* * *

When Gidley King, a British sailor, first gave Australia's Aborigines some wine to drink, they blew it out of their mouths. There was no wine, and no civilization in Australia helping to prove the point of this book's thesis. However, James Busby's book, *A Treatise on the Culture of the Vine and the Art of Making Wine*, helped Australia become a wine growing, and a wine drinking British colony. He's considered Australia's wine father. Soon, vines also were in Tasmania, and then on to New Zealand.

There was still confusion about Australian wines well into the 20th Century. Their Riesling grown in the Hunter Valley was actually made from the Sémillon grape. In the Clare Valley, their Riesling turned out to be the Crouchen grape, which is now nearly extinct from the Pyrenees area of France. However, it can still be found in South Africa. Syrah, or as Australians called it, Shiraz, is correctly named, and is now the most widely exported red wine from Australia. Shiraz helped Australia get its name spread throughout the wine-drinking world. Shiraz, a Persian city, may have been what that ancient civilization called their red wine when they first traded it around the Mediterranean, and into southern France.

Australia's Victoria region had its own gold rush just 36 months after California's 1849 epidemic of gold-fever. Vineyards had been planted all over the eastern and southern parts of the country by then, and the making of wine became a hobby of many Australian medical doctors. The most famous is Dr. Christopher Penfold. His family owned the eponymous winery until 1962, but his creation of Grange-Hermitage, now just Grange, is still thought to be Australia's premier Grand Cru! As wine progressed, so did the nation of Australia as it built a civilization the Aborigines could have never even imagined.

By the mid-20th Century, New Zealand was selling millions of bottles of Sauvignon Blanc, and expanded their Pinot Noir acreage to help satisfy North America's and Great Britain's fascination with the grape that France's Burgundy region had made world famous.

Pinot Noir grew in popularity from the Middle Ages, right up to today. With Pinot Noir's vast new worldwide plantings, it may well become the most popular wine well into the 21st Century.

*   *   *

Roughly 13,000 years ago, much of North America was covered with ice. By 11,000 years ago, the ice was withdrawing, leaving the Great Lakes, and thousands of other smaller ponds to help irrigate the rebirth of vegetation that included wild grapevines. There were four cycles of warm weather, and icy glaciations, over the past 600,000 years that can be confirmed. As the most recent Ice Age cleared, humans were actively hunting mastodon, moose and caribou, fishing and foraging, and building tiny villages along the trading routes from Maine down to Tennessee, and beyond.

These early North Americans never became interested in fermented grape juice. They may have accidentally found some very primitive wine naturally fermented in crevasses of rocks where wild grapes may have fallen, and fermented with their own wild yeasts. The resulting liquid, from a lesser species of grapes, did not encourage any further interest in it as was happening far across the planet in areas around the Black Sea.

As the continent continued to warm, the local natives grew in number and developed larger tribes that lived harmoniously with nature. These were the first Transcendentalists; they were a people who aspired to live within the confines of nature, and transcend themselves above earthly desires and stay with the basic necessities. These first North Americans found no need for wine, and never build the vast civilizations where wine was grown, made, consumed, and traded. The present man-helped global warming may just be delaying the next Ice Age, because nothing can block the cycles of nature.

From the time Leif Eriksson called North America *Vinland*, because of all the indigenous grape vines growing through the forest, until the *Vitis vinifera* species could enhance the quality of the wines made there, civilization paralleled the growth of the wine industry. Before this European species of grape was planted on American rootstock to save it from the native Phylloxera aphid because it had no immunity toward it, American wine growers had only the far lesser *Vitis labrusca* species to use in making wine. In the southern states of the new nation, wine was made from the Scuppernong grapes, which are in the *Vitis rotundifolia* species. Aside from a short period of popularity when it was sold under the Virginia Dare label, it was, in all honesty, not a civilized drink.

In 1854, Henry Wadsworth Longfellow composed an "Ode to Catawba Wine". This native grape made an interesting sparkling wine from the Ohio and Missouri states, but soon after the Civil War, the new nation began to grow, and expand its modern civilization, along with its knowledge and desire for better wines. Crossing native grapes with European grapes created a selection of hybrids that were an improvement, but still unequal to the quality of the Old World wines. Learning which *vinifera* grape was best suited to what areas, has made America a wine-drinking nation, and now, into the 21st Century, the world's largest wine consumer, and most productive civilization. Although the country does not consider itself an Empire of any sorts, it does have the responsibility of policing the world's conflicts, and it provides aid when fire, flood, or famine strikes anywhere. This new winemaking society, once again, continues expanding the history of civilization.

In the 1800's, Agoston Haraszthy provided innumerable species of European grape varieties to help make California North America's wine focal point. The curious Zinfandel grape is thought to be one of his unique interjections into California's vast world of wine. Today, all 50 states make, consume, and sell wine.

Just as the Old World was making great progress in its wine productions, and its advanced civilizations experimented with social freedoms through democracy, the Phylloxera epidemic hit Europe, and nearly wiped out the entire wine industry. When the newest Free Trade agreements were boosting wine sales to new heights, but just after the plague of odium was won, the disease from America spread everywhere. It took some time to figure out that American roots had evolved immunity to it, so by graphing American rootstocks onto the classic European varieties, traditional grapes could continue to be grown, and made into the best wines possible. Scientific research methods learned during the Age of the Enlightenment guided the modern civilizations of the West in finding solutions to these problems. Louis Pasteur cured the microorganism problem that caused spoilage, and copper-sulfate spray kept the mildew in check. Oenology continued to advance so that the 21ˢᵗ Century wines might be the best ever produced.

Champagne, Bordeaux, Burgundy, and Rhone wines lived through a Miraculous Age during the late 1800's with Portugal, Spain, Italy, and Germany quickly following suit. After both World Wars were decided, wine growth, and an expanded consumption, Western nations were ready to lead the world into a new prosperity with better living standards for all the people of civilized wine-drinking nations, more so than ever before.

During the Phylloxera crisis in Europe, the French planted vast vineyards in their colony of Morocco. Good wine is still produced there, but their dominant religious restrictions prevent them from consumption. It's a classic example of a Third-world nation *not* using wine, as it's been used down through the ages, to advance their life-style and civilization.

*   *   *

South American wines from Chile, Argentina, and Uruguay all have samples that fit into modern world class Grand Cru selections. South America wines, with major investments from Spain, France, Germany, and the United States, are being produced in societies that foster freedom and growth, and are building the world's newest civilizations as they build their vineyards, wineries, and expand their wine trade. Sound familiar? It should, because it's been noted throughout the chapters of this book how wine has aided, and built civilizations, since mankind came away from hunting and gathering, and decided to settle down to plant grape vines along with its other grains. Settling to grow grapes, and make wine, forced these early people to domesticate animals to help them work the vineyards, and as also to become a local food source. Life got easier.

When the conquistadors first landed in South America, they had Jesuit, and Franciscan priests, with them. They also carried barrels of wine to use for their Mass. They came to conquer and convert. These new 17th Century Crusaders understood that vines had to be planted so that wine could be made on location, because it took far too long for ships to bring in the necessary supplies that were used in every daily Mass, and that was used during the forced conversions of the local natives. The Spaniards came to Christianize, and steal the gold. Ironically, during native rebellions, these so-called savages, many times forced the priests, and conquistadors, to drink molten gold, the item they desired so much, as a torturing execution just as the invaders forced the natives to drink the liquid wines when they were forced to partake Communion.

Argentina had the largest South American plantings, and is

still among the world's top producers. Then as now, Chile made the best South American wines. Uruguay, by the 20th Century, was producing European-stylized wines because of all the immigrant wine-makers. Brazil is expanding it wine production, but is still making mostly sweeter wines to satisfy its large and poorly educated population. Today, as it did in the last century, it makes sweeter wines of lesser quality, but Brazil is quickly changing its culture, and its wines, to suit a worldwide, more modern, civilized taste. For a long time, Brazil made wine from native grapes like Concord, and Delaware, and later from the hybrid Isabella grape, in the same manner as the Eastern part of the United States did. Now, both areas know better, and *Vitis vinifera* grapes are producing the finest wines of the New World.

Peru, Bolivia, and Colombia, are now also making wine, but they are still in the earliest stages of wine development as is their development of stable social societies. Over and over again, history shows wine progression advancing hand-in-hand with civilization.

There were many indigenous grapes growing in South America, but there is no evidence that the Aztecs, or the Incas, ever produced wine from them. They had other intoxicating drinks, and possibly had no reason to experiment with wine production. Although their societies were expansive, they made no major advancements in civilization as the Middle Eastern civilizations had done while their wine trade funded their research into mathematics, architecture, medicine, engineering, art, music, philosophy, and literature.

Cortés put in vines in the 1550's, and Pizarro followed during the 1560's. So much wine was made in South America, that by the end of the 1600's, Spain put restrictions on importing New World wine to protect their homeland production.

Wine is now produced on every continent except Antarctica. South America continues to make better and better wines. North American wines, even those from Mexico and Canada, can be found everywhere. California, Washington State, and Oregon wines, compete evenly with classic European examples. The later part of the 20th Century saw Eastern Europe expand it wine production, and began making wines in the modern style for international trading and improved sales. The 21st Century is viewing ancient China as the next civilization to be changed by wine.

*   *   *

We know that wine was imported into China from the west in the second century A.D. Research also shows that the Chinese procured grape seeds from Uzbekistan around 130 B.C. Remember, that Uzbekistan probably had a grape, and wine influence, from Georgia and other Black Sea areas as far back as the Stone Age. By the mid 600's A.D., the Chinese were making a white wine from a grape called *Maru*. That data simply shows that China has long been interested in wine. Because of its fundamental philosophies, China had rejected any western influence, and progress, to remain isolated. However, that has all changed since the end of World War Two.

Because China's extreme population needs rice to feed its people, they have restricted rice-wine production, and have turned back to grape wine similar to what their ancestors had sought out. Because China has so many micro-climates in so many different areas, it's a very large nation, they can, and are, planting vineyards with *Vitis vinifera* grapes best suited to each area. Modern Europe is investing heavily into future Chinese wine just as modern Chinese have been buying vineyards, and numerous Chateaus in France. There's already well over 407,500 acres of vineyards in provinces north of the Yangtze River. Over-cropping, and poor quality production is quickly fading, and the new higher quality wines are being accepted in Europe as well as at home. It's a similar story to the growth of Californian wines.

Moët Hennessy started in 2009 to produce a high-end Chinese wine, and today their new Chinese red wine, called *Ao Yun*, sells for $250 a bottle. It comes from the Yunnan Province near Tibet in a place where Jesuit missionaries, back in the 1800's, first planted grapes. Once again, wine, religion, and civilization's advancement are tied together. China is already the 5th largest producer of wine worldwide, and is rapidly planting more and better vineyards to satisfy local demand. Even though Chinese locals drink only one-tenth of what American drinkers do, that will change just as North Americans moved from beer, and whiskeys, toward more wine at the end of the 20th Century. Westerners are now investing heavily in Chinese wine for the future.

Chinese Professor Li Demci, lectured at the 2017 ProWein Conference in Düsseldorf, Germany, on the vast plantings of the Marselan grape in China. Marselan is a cross of the Cabernet Sauvignon and Grenache grapes. It was created by Professor Paul Truel in 1961 in southern France. The grape produces small berries, which is better for juice-to-skin ratios, makes large bunches, and has excellent resistance to diseases. It's been planted in Brazil and Uruguay too, but its future seems to be in China where nearly 8,000 acres have already been planted. Old China is quickly becoming a world leader with regards to changes in the wine world.

*　　*　　*

The 18th, 19th, and 20th Centuries saw a repetition of wine expansion tied to civilizations' growth, and advancement, in the same way it had advanced and grew ever since the Late Stone Age. What had happen in Egypt, Greece, and all the other early civilizations repeated the process. Civilizations evolved as long as wine was being made and traded. Since the Age of Enlightenment, our scientific methods have increased the rate of social and scientific growth, and much of civilization is better for it. It was wine that caused the creation of great civilizations, and not because of civilization was wine created. Wine has always offered a proclivity for contemplation. Sadly, even in our modern world there is no algorithm to explain the pleasure, and importance, of wine.

The 21st Century, and beyond, will see many social, religious, and economic difficulties, but as long as wine is made available, mankind will continue to build advanced civilizations. After all, it was wine that caused our species to move out of its caves, build villages, then cities, and eventually, as shown, it was wine that was the source of civilization.

SUMMARY

The time period we've just covered, from our most recent Cro-Magnon human ancestors up to our modern Homo sapiens, which means "wise man", is but a nanosecond with regards to life on our planet.

I hope that just enough proof has been presented to permit further conversations, and debate, as to whether it was *wine* that fostered civilization, or is wine, as it is usually thought to be, just a consequence of the social development that advanced ancient societies, and their vast civilizations. A society's wealth permitted the building of roads, aquifers, canals to irrigate, and temples where festivals could be held. That wealth came from trade, and wine was civilization's key trading commodity. It took wise men to do this.

Even during the Stone Age, men needed to trade their stone weapons for flints, furs for food, and most likely, a little poorly homemade wine in exchange for some basic necessity of life. Once larger tribes settled, and could plant grapevines, they could produce better and larger quantities of wine to trade. Very early on, it was for the tin they needed to add to copper so they could make bronze. The strength of bronze provided better weapons, and also the tools they needed to build larger buildings and protective forts. These very early entrepreneurs traded wine to get the tin.

With better tools, agriculture expanded and populations grew. More and more people wanted wine. The best examples of each vintage went to the leaders and priests whose education provided them the ability to appreciate wine's meditative qualities as well as its health benefits. The poorest quality wines were given to the lower, uneducated, superstitious classes, who drank it to ease their pain from tedious labor. Any wine the lowest class found repulsive went to the slaves.

By the time mankind entered the Iron Age, wine-growing techniques, and its basic quality, had greatly improved. It could now be traded for more expensive necessary items, and even for some luxuries. Societies built larger empires as progressive, more scientific, civilizations emerged.

From the time our species first stood upright, walked across the African savanna, and migrated north to Europe and to the Middle East, then all the way into India and China, is but a blink of the eye with regards to the period of time that life has been on the earth. This evolution of humans took nearly four million years, but mankind, as we know it, only started to advance after the last Ice Age, or just ten to twelve thousands years ago. Dinosaurs ruled the earth for over 150 million years. Maybe the usage of "nanosecond" for our existence is much too long?

*   *   *

The Mesozoic period started 248 million years ago and continued up to 65 million years ago when it was ended, scientists believe, by an asteroid hitting the earth. This Mesozoic, meaning "middle" period, is divided into three eras of time each so long that it's hard to conceive. The Triassic period viewed the first few dinosaurs on the land, but the oceans were filled with millions of both small and enormous new creatures.

The Jurassic period, that we know from the movie, *Jurassic Park*, went from 208 million years down to just over 146 million years ago. During this period, huge herbivores were food for massive carnivores. The *Archaeopteryx*, which is the first bird, evolved during this Jurassic period.

The Cretaceous period, 146 million years flowing down to just 65 million years ago, saw the continental shapes, and their locations on the globe, settle into the shape they now look like, and also where they are located today. Mammals, for the first time, increased in population and variety. More feathered birds fought for space in the skies with flying reptiles. Tyrannosaurus Rex terrorized all the animal groups, but he too, was eliminated during the asteroid strike. The next period would be one where mammals would dominate, and from which, mankind would evolve. Brawn was still the most valued trait until the brain of mankind enlarged, and became the masterpiece of evolution. Primates date back to 60 millions years ago during the Paleocene period, but all we're concerned with is the most recent nine or ten thousand years, covering the time since wine began to be sought out, and civilization evolved.

*   *   *

Permit me to summarize, in reverse order, what we've just read; showing that wine was the source of civilization. The past three centuries have seen the greatest improvements in viticulture since the Roman era. Modern wines are better than ever, can be shipped anywhere, and age well when made to do so. Wine consumption worldwide is now at its highest level ever, and wine is seen as the most civilized drink in the educated world. The anonymous slogan of the Knights of the Vine, "Water separates the people of the world; wine unites them," has been seen in print since 1971, but goes way back to some wine lover in the 19th Century.

The Aborigines stayed isolated; they made no wine. Since Leif Eriksson, and later on, Columbus, the New World was fascinated with wine, but was much slower to improve it as the Old World had done. The New World stayed less civilized, and less progressive, until its use of wine expanded. South America is currently seeing the flowering of an artistic and progressive society similar to what Post-Roman Europe developed with its wine.

The greatest strides have been made in the quality of wine since Louis Pasteur showed that science goes hand-in-hand with the modernization of wine. The Incas and the Aztecs had neither the science, nor the grapes, necessary to produce quality wine. Neither their drinks, nor their civilizations, advanced quickly. Their North American cousins, the native tribes of North America, were also devoid of winemaking skills or wine knowledge, and never developed Middle Eastern-like civilizations that flourished with profits from wine.

China, one of the oldest civilizations, is at last progressing into a modern civilization at the same time as they are expanding their grape plantings and wine consumption. Few nations or societies have made such a rapid growth in oenology since the Age of the Enlightenment.

During the mid-1600's, and throughout the 1700's, continuous petty wars slowed European nations from any rapid growth, but their desire for wine, and wine-trading companies, kept all the grape growers and winemakers united. They may be thought of as the first EU, or European Union, organizers. Even today, Europe's wine makers sour when political differences among its members threaten their potential wine trading.

After the improvements made in glassware, the development of *brandewijn*, and in the shipping and cellaring of wine all advanced, society progressed. The Dutch got rich off the wine improvements made in Germany, France, Italy, and Spain. They even helped Portugal become a world player. Great Britain's vast desire for strong wine encouraged Portugal, Madeira, the Canary Islands, and the Spanish Sherry district, all to grow and prosper.

As the Moslems withdrew from Eastern and Central Europe, those places could once again produce desirable wines, which in turn advanced their civilizations. Hungary is a prime example of this wine revival. This was during the same period that France's Bordeaux vineyards were expanded. In no time at all, Bordeaux wines became world famous, setting a standard for quality that has lasted until the present day.

A Summary of wine's importance during the Middle Ages necessitates noting Charlemagne. The Dark Ages, following Rome's decline, set back mankind's advancements in both the Arts and the Sciences. The only flickering of light during this endless night for culture, was when wine was consumed; relaxing human stress, enhancing the mediocre food, sanitizing whatever it touched without anyone knowing it, and providing a humble, but definitive, item for trade. Wine, its production, and its sales, made it possible to prevent a complete blackout. Wine was tied to every thinking man's history, and only those involved with wine made any progress during these dimly lighted centuries. The screw press used to crush grapes was really a return to what earlier people had already developed. Wine provided the revenue to build all the previous civilizations, and wine would do so once again.

The Visigoths, Vandals, and Goths, who all ransacked the civilized Roman Empire, would drink wine, but made no effort to plant vineyards, harvest grapes, or make wine for a commodity to trade. This Dark Age period, a time without an expansion of wine knowledge, should be evidence enough to prove the thesis of this work, but to win a debate on the topic, a full history, however succinct, was needed to convince the doubtful.

The Moors, who did expand some of the societies that they conquered, were smart enough to see the value of wine, and they used it to fund their constructions. The Muslim areas that completely prohibited wine and vineyards, fell into decline, and have remained so until the present time. El Cid's liberation of winegrowing Spain, the Church's need of wine to perform its holy rites, and the merchants of an expanding Venice, rekindled enough light to show civilized man a way out of the Dark and Middle Ages.

*   *   *

Continuing backward in time, we ask, was it really wine that was the catalyst that developed civilizations? It can be answered by looking back no further than the Roman Empire. Some of the greatest agriculture and viniculture experts of all time were Romans. Cato, of course, and especially Columella, who provided the Romans with detailed writings about how to improve their vineyards, and then produce better quality wines. Columella came from Cádiz in Roman Spain. His writings provide us with the most data on how important wine was to the rapidly expanding early Roman Empire.

The Romans taught the benefit of rotating crops, which if we'd remembered it, would have prevented our disastrous Dust Bowls of the 1930's. Romans set up Inns along their 51,000 miles of roadways so travelers could refresh themselves with healthy wine instead of bacteria infected water. They also were the first civilization to rank the quality of their wines placing *Falernum* at the top, and they taught that aged wines developed more complexities, and provided a drink that demanded contemplation to appreciate all of its subtle qualities. Rome's classifications were more specific than how the earlier Egyptians ranked vintage quality.

Pliny recorded the Roman story of expansions, and he told how trading wine provided the wealth the Romans needed to build an Empire. He also provided the records of what all the earlier Greeks had done when they transplanted the grapevine everywhere they traveled. Wine kept the conquering Roman soldiers healthy and able to fight just as it had provided healthy Greek armies for Alexander the Great.

When Homer wrote about the island of Crete, about nine centuries before Christ, he told about a time a thousand years earlier: the war with Troy. Homer penned about a rich land with so many people they could not be counted, and of a place with ninety cities. "There is a land called Crete, in the midst of the wine-dark sea," wrote Homer. It seems that he's calling the Mediterranean a dark-colored sea as we might call the far north Atlantic, but the Mediterranean is a bright aqua-blue color, and around most of the

Greek islands, it's nearly a sky-blue, far from wine-dark. He was referring to, I believe, a place that traded so much red wine that the stains on the ships and the spills into the harbors turned the water a dark wine color. Homer is proving to us that wine was being made and traded as the most advanced and richest civilization of the era had wine as its source of growth and progress. *Ho Pontos* is what the Greeks called the Mediterranean, meaning a Roadway or a Passage. It was their thoroughfare to surpassing the Phoenicians as they spread the grape vine all around the Mediterranean, and founded settlements where vines could be grown and even more wine be made.

It was the Romans who spread the newest religion, Christianity. After Emperor Constantine converted, his mandate that the Roman Empire would all be Christian meant that wine would be needed everywhere so that the rites of the Christian Mass could be enacted. In summarizing this thesis, it's very important to recall all of the religions and theological concepts that mankind had developed since he first developed the ability to talk, and then asked questions about the role he played in his earthly environment.

Jewish and Christian dedication to wine as a spiritual symbol, and to the grape vine that taught them about resurrection each new spring, is obvious. But seeing how the Jews got their legends from Babylon, from many of the Egyptian rituals, and even from earlier Sumerian customs, helps tied us all together as we study the growth and expansion of civilization. From the time of Pharaoh Amenhotep IV's ruling that there was but one god, down through the ages to today's theological concepts, wine has never been left out of spiritual rituals.

The Dionysian stories, first devised to help explain everything from seasonal changes, to offering the wishful concept of another life after death, have influenced every sector of modern theologies. This Dionysus, the god of wine, and all his rituals, still influence modern society.

*   *   *

Going even further backwards from the early Iron Age deep into the start of the Bronze Age helps us immediately see wine's major influence in the development of civilizations. The Greek Thucydides wrote in the 5th Century B.C. that the people around the Mediterranean rose from Barbarism as they learned to cultivate olives and the grapevine. By the late Bronze Age, or about 1200 B.C., when every stone tool was replaced with a bronze instrument, wine had started being shipped everywhere. The profits from the wine trade aided greatly in the building of larger fleets, warehouses, and business districts that expanded city limits. Amphorae were designed to be fermentation tanks, and other smaller amphorae were used as vessels to transport the finished wine across the land, and over the seas.

Early writers from Homer to Aristophanes sang the praises of wine. By the time the Greeks settled and planted vines in Sicily and Malta, they were using large copper fermenting tanks. It has been recorded that wine had been a major concern for mankind for over four, five, and even six thousand years. More recent studies, stemming from the Anthropology Department at the University of Pennsylvania, are showing that residue from fermented grapes that made wine go back to even 8,000 years. It's been the conjecture of this work to project that wine is even older, and most likely was experimented with as far back as 9,000 or more years ago. Wine may have been first fermented as soon as our cavemen ancestors could stop migrating as hunter-gathers, and settle to grow some vines with their grains, as they built the first human settlements.

Wine making has been confirmed in what's considered the first city, *Catal Hüyük* in what is now modern Turkey. Carbon dating has confirmed even older residue of fermented grape pips in Georgia, and in what was called Anatolia, along the shores of the Black Sea. That research puts the birth of winemaking at 8,000 years old, or during the Stone Age. That out-dates, by ten centuries, the Chinese fermentation of a rice-honey wine made for their nobility. I suspect that men were settling to make wine during the Neolithic Age, 9,000 B.C. on Crete as well as in *Catal Hüyük*.

It is easy to find readings about the Phoenicians, the Hittites, and even the older Canaanites, who traveled with wine and grapevines just as the 15th Century Spaniards did in their journeys to South America. Even reports of the expanding Persian Empire record trading wine and commerce flourishing. It is much harder, however, to find any records of how the *sylvestris,* the wild vines growing in the forest, were cultivated into the modern species of *Vitis vinifera.* The Egyptian wine containers that date "year 9" and "year 31", found in King Tut's tomb, most certainly were vastly improved vintages over what the first humans made in their clay pots buried into the floors of their stick huts. It's pretty clear that Noah simply copied the idea of planting a vineyard, and was not the first person to ever do so.

If there were wild grape-like berries, and natural wild yeasts, living during the Age of the Dinosaurs in the Mesozoic Period, those berries, most surely, must have fallen after ripening. If any of those grape clusters fell into a rocky crevasse, they would have naturally fermented into a most primitive type of wine. Dinosaurs then, 248 million years ago, would have been the earliest animals to have ever tasted wine. Realistically, we can only review legends like that of Jamsheed, whose jar full of grapes fermented accidently, and the resulting alcoholic beverage was first experienced by the damsel who tried to poison herself. What is so interesting is the fact that so many ancient stories try to relate how wine first came about. They all tell how gods like Dionysus gave them the gift of wine. Whether from the tales of Gilgamesh or pre-Iliad stories, men have always found wine so important that they needed to discover its source.

Every great civilization stemmed from making and trading wine. Knowing this should, I hope, make every student of wine, and therefore every lover of all the civilized arts that project from wine, never stop learning about it. The history of wine is the way to learn about ourselves: our evolution, our beliefs, and our goals for the future. It was mankind's quest for wine that led him to end a hunter-gathering existence, and settle to plant grapevines, harvest, and then ferment the grapes he grew into wine. He drank it to ease his pain, and as a medicine; he enhanced his clay pots and artwork with grapevines, and he traded wine to obtain all the materials necessary to advance and build civilizations.

Through expanding our knowledge of wine, we can open the doors to more culture. Wine is, without a doubt, the source of all civilization. *In Vino Veritas.*

BIBLIOGRAPHY

Chapters One and Two

Adkins, L., Empires of the Plain: Henry Rawlinson and the Lost Languages of Babylon (2004, New York)

Amerine, M.A. & Singleton, V.L., Wine (1976, Davis)

Andrews, R.C., On the Trail of Ancient Man (1930, New York)

Bass, G.F., Oldest known Shipwreck Revels Splendors of the Bronze Age, National Geographic (Dec. 1987)

Capart, J., Thebes (1926, London)

Chardin, Sir J., Travels into Persia and the East Indies through the Black Sea and the Country of Colchis (1686, London).

Charpentier, L., Le Mystèrie du Vin (1981, Paris)

Cowan, A.R., Master Clues in World History (1914, London)

Darby, W.J., Food: the Gift of Osiris (1977, London)

Dragadze, T., Banqueting in Soviet Georgia "Private dissertation, St. Anthony's College, Oxford"

Durant, W., *The Story of Civilization: Part I*, Simon and Schuster (1954, New York)

Herodotus, The Histories of Herodotus of Halicarnassus translated by Harry Carter (1962, Oxford)

Huart, C., *Ancient Persia and Iranian Civilization*, translated by M.R. Dobie, (1996, New York & London)

Hyams, E., Dionysus: A Social History of the Wine Vine (1965, London)

Johnson, H., Wine Companion 2nd ed. (1978, London)
— World Atlas of Wine 3rd ed. (1985, London)
— Vintage: The Story of Wine (1989, London)

Lang, D.M., Armenia: Cradle of Civilization (1970, London)

Laufer, B., Chinese Contributions to the History of Civilization in Ancient Iran: the Grape-Vine, in Sino-Iranica (1919, Chicago)

Lesko, L.H., King Tut's Wine Cellar (1977, Berkeley)

Leonard, W.E., Gilgamesh: Epic of Old Babylonia (1934, New York)

Maspero, G., History of Egypt, Chaldea, Syria, Babylonia, and Assyria, Vol. II *Edition de Luxe* (1903, London)

Maclean, F., To Caucasus (1976, London)

Macqueen, J.G., The Hittites and Their Contemporaries in Asia Minor (1986, London)

Ramishvili, R., New Archaeological Evidence on the History of Viticulture in Georgia, in Matsne No.2 (1983, Tbilisi)

Renard, G., Life and Work in Prehistoric Times (1929, New York)

Rickard, T.A., Man and Metals (1932, New York)

Rostovtzeff, M., A History of the Ancient World (1930, Oxford)

Smith, G.E., Human History (1929, New York)

Smith, J.M.P., The Origin and History of Hebrew Lay (1931, Chicago)

Smith, R., Religion of the Semites (2017, New York)

Strabo, The Geography of Strabo (2014, Lulu.com)

Sykes, P.M., History of Persia (1915, London)

Wagner, P., Grapes into Wine (1974, New York)

Younger, W., Gods, Men and Wine (1966, London)

Chapters Three, Four and Five

Allen, G., Evolution of the Idea of God (1897, New York)

Aquinas, T., *Summa Theologica. Part Three, Treatise on the Sacraments, Vol 18 & 19* (1932, London)

Arrian of Nicomedia, Anabasis of Alexander, and Indica (1893, London)

Boardman, J., The Greeks Overseas (1980, London)

Besant, A., India (1923, Madras)

Breasted, J.H., Ancient Records of Egypt (1906, Chicago)
— The Conquest of Civilization (1926, New York)
— The Development of Religion and Thought in Ancient Egypt (1912, New York)

Bowen, J.C.E., Poems from the Persian (1948, Essex) Chilver *Cisalpine Gaul* (1944, Oxford)

Braue, D.A., Māyā in Radhakrishnan's Thought, *Six Meanings Other than Illusion,*

(1984, Delhi)

Carpenter, E., Pagan and Christian Creeds (1920, New York)

Culpepper, R. Alan, "The Gospel of Luke" in The New Interpreter's Bible (Nashville: Abingdon, 2002)

Davis, W.S., Influence of Wealth in Imperial Rome, (1910, Eugene)

Deiss, J., Herculaneum (1968, London)

Delaporte, L., Mesopotamia (1925, London)

DeMorgan, J., Prehistoric Man (1925, New York)

Dhirendra, K.B., Wine in Ancient India, (Calcutta, 1927)

Doane, T.W., Bible Myths and their Parallels in Other Religions (1882, New York)

Drower, E.S., Water into Wine (1956, London)

Duncan Jones, R., The Economy of the Roman Empire (1982, Cambridge)

Durant, W., Our Oriental Heritage: The Story of Civilization Part I (1954, New York)

Eddy, S., The Challenge of the East (1931, New York)

Encyclopaedia Judaica (1972, Jerusalem)

Erman, A., Life in Egypt (1894, London)

Fraser, P., Ptolemaic Alexandria (1972, Oxford)

Granet, M., Chinese Civilization (1930, New York)

Gowen, H.H., An Outline History of Japan (2001, Cambridge)

Harper. R.F. (ed), Assyrian and Babylonian Literature (1904, New York)

Hamidullah, M., Introduction to Islam (1980, Luton)

Hammond, N.G.L. & Scullard, H.H., editors, The Oxford Classical Dictionary (1979, Oxford)

Huart, C., Ancient Persian and Iranian Civilization (1927, New York)

Herodotus, The History of Herodotus of Halicarnassus translated by Harry Carter (1962, Oxford)

Hume, R.E., The Thirteen Principal Upanishads, *Translated from the Sanskrit,* (1921, London)

Jastrow, M.J., The Civilization of Babylonia and Assyria (1915, Philadelphia)

Johnson, P., A History of Christianity (1976, London)

Khayyam, O., *Rubaiyat* translated by E. Fitzgerald (1968, London)

Kramer, S.N., Sumerian Mythology: A Study of Spiritual and Literary Achievements in the Third Millennium B.C. (1961, Philadelphia)

Duham, W., Reuters: "Drinking age: oldest evidence of wine-making found near Tbilisi" (Nov. 13, 2017,Washington)

The Koran, translated by N.J. Dawood (1947, London)

Lippert, J., Evolution of Culture (1931, New York)

Lubbock, J. Sir, The Origin of Civilization (1912, London)

Lucia, S.P., A History of Wine as Therapy (1963, New York)

Mason, O.T., Origins of Invention (1899, New York)

Maspero, G., The Passing of the Empires (1900, London)

McCuistion, P.R., Warner, C. & Viljoen. F.P., 2014, "The influence of Greek drama on Matthew's Gospel", HTS Theological Studies 70(1), Art.#2024,http://dx.doi.org/10.4102/hts.v70i1.2024

McGovern, Patrick E., "Beginning of Winemaking in France," (2013, Philadelphia) www.penn.museum/sites/biomoleculararchaeology/

Moret, A. and Davy, G., From Tribe to Empire (1926, New York)

Müller-Lyer, F., History of Social Development (1921, New York)

Muller, F.M., The Six Systems of Indian Philosophy

(1919, Varanasi, India)

Nag, K., Greater India (1926, Calcutta)

Nestor The Annalist, The Russian Primary Chronicle Laurentian, text translated by S.H. Cross and O.P. Sherbowitz-Wetzor (1953, Cambridge, MA)

— Ancient Wine: The Search for the Origins of Viniculture (2006, Princeton)

The New Encyclopedia Britannica, 15th ed. (2010, Chicago)

Osborn, H.F., Men of the Old Stone Age (1915, New York)

Petrie, Sir W.M. F., The Revolutions of Civilizations (1911, London)

Peyre, C., *La Cisalpine Gauloise du IIIe au Ier Siècle Avant J-C* (1970, Paris)

Polatanyi, K., Trade and Market in the Early Empires (1963, Glencoe)

Purcell, N., Wine and Wealth in Ancient Italy, in Journal of Roman Studies (1986)

Rahim, Z., 6,000-Year-Old Wine Residue Found in Sicilian Cave, (2017, CNN) http://www.cnn.com/2017/08/30/europe/ sicily-6000-year-old-wine-discovered/?iid=0b_homepage_ deskrecommended_pool

Ratzel, F., History of Mankind (1896, London)

Rawlinson, G. (ed), *Herodotus* (1862, London)

Reinach, S., Orpheus: A History of Religions (1930, New York)

Renan, E., History of the People of Israel (1888, New York)

Renfrew, C., The Emergence of Civilization (1972, London)

Rice, D.S., Deacon or Drink: Some Paintings from Samarra Re-Examined, in Arabica (1958)

Rostovtzell, M.I., Daedalus, Vol. 103, No.1 Twentieth-Century Classics Revisited, "The Social and Economic History of the Roman Empire" (1974, Boston)

Ruck, C.A.P., The Wild and the Cultivated: Wine in Euripides' Bacchae, in Journal of Ethno-Pharmacology (1985)

Schäfer, H. and Andrae, W., *Die Kunst des alten Orients* (1925, Berlin)

Schep, L., "Mystery of Alexander the Great's Death Solved? Ruler was killed by toxic wine claim scientists" (2014, GMT) www.independent.co.uk/news.science/mystery-of-alexander-the-greats-death-solved-ruler-was-killed-by-toxic-claim-scientists-9054625.html

Sidhanta, N.K., The Heroic Age of India, A Comparative Study, *The History of Civilization* (1996, New York)

Smith, A.H., Chinese Characteristics (1894, New York)

Smith, J.M.P., The Origin and History of Hebrew Law (1931, Chicago)

Smith, W. R., The Religion of the Semites (1889, New York)

Sollas, W. J., Ancient Hunters (1924, New York)

Sparkes, B.A., *Kottabos,* In Archaeology (1960)

Sprengling, M., The Alphabet: Its Rise and Development from the Sinai Inscriptions, Oriental Institute Publications (1938, Chicago)

St.Fleur, N., Trilobites, New York Times, Wine from Prehistoric Georgia with an 8,000 Year-Old Vintage (Nov. 13, 2017, New York)

Stanislawski, D., Dionysus Westward: Early Religion and the Economic Geography of Wine, in The Geographical Review (Oct. 1975)
— Dark Age Contributions to the Mediterranean Way of Life, in Annals of the Association of American Geographers (1973)

Summer, W.G., Folkways (1906, Boston)

Tabouis, G.R., Nebuchadnezzar (1931, New York)

Toynbee, A., A Study of History, (London, 1934)

Thorndike, L., Short History of Civilization (1926, New York)

Tylor, E.B., Anthropology (1906, New York)
— Primitive Culture (1889, New York)

Vinogradoff, P. Sir, Outlines of Historical Jurisprudence (1922, Oxford)

Walker, B.L., A Concise History of Japan (2015, Cambridge)

White, K.D., Roman Farming (1979, London)

Williams, J. A., Themes of Islamic Civilization (1971, Berkeley)

Williams, S.W., The Middle Kingdom (1895, New York)

Wilken, R., The Christians as the Roman Saw Them (1984, New Haven)

Woolley, C.L., The Sumerians, (1927, New York)

Yerkes, R.K., Sacrifice in Greek and Roman Religions and Early Judaism

(1953, London)

Chapter Six

Ambrosi, H. & Becker, H., *Der Deutschen Wein* (1978, Munich)

Barty-King, H., Tradition of English Wine (1977, Oxford)

Bazin, J.F., *Le Clos de Vougeot* (1987, Paris)

Berlow, R.K., The Disloyal Grape: the Agrarian Crisis of Late 14th Century Burgundy, in *Agricultural History* (1982)

Childe V. G., The Dawn of European Civilization (1925, New York)

Dion, R., *Histoire de la Vigne et du Vin en France* (1959, Paris)

Forgeot, P., *Origines du Vignoble Bourguignon* (1972, Paris)

Freeden, M.H., *Festung Marienberg* 1982, urzburg)

Garcia, J. J. E., Rules and Regulations for Drinking Wine in Frances Eiximenis' *Terc del Crestis* (1384) in *Teaditio* (1976)

Hutchinson, V. J., Bacchus in Roman Britain (9186, Oxford)

De Kerdeland, J., *Histoire des Vins du France* (1964, Paris)

Dumay, R., (ed), *Le Vin de Bourgogne* (1976, Paris)

Lachiver, M., *Vin, Vignes et Vignerons* (1988, Paris)

Langenbach, A., German Wine and Vines (1962, London)

Lucia, S. P., A History of Wine as Therapy (1963, New York)

Mitenbuler, R., What Did Wine Taste Like Thousands of Years Ago? *Dinking in History*, drinks.seriouseats.com

Peacock, D.P.S., The Rhine and the Problem of Gaulish Wine in Roman Britain, in *Roman Shipping and Trade*, ed. H. Cleere, (1978, London)

Piggott, S., (ed), France Before the Romans (1974, London)

Remouard, Y., *Le Vin Vieux au Moyen Age*, in *Annales du Midi* (1964) — *La Consommation des Grands Vins du Bourbonnais et de Bourgogne a la Cour Pontificale d'Avignon*, in *Annales de Bourgogne* (1982)

Sealey, P. & Davies, G.M., Falernum in Colchester, in *Britannia* (1984)

Seward, D., Monks and Wine (1979, London)

Sigerist, H.E., The Earliest Printed Book on Wine (1934) The History of Wine: Sulphorous Acid Used in Wineries for 500 Years, in German Wine Review #2 (1986, *Neustadt an der Weinstrasse*)

Tchernia, A., Italian Wine in Gaul at the End of the Republic, in *Trade in the Ancient Economy*, (eds) P. Garnsey, C.R.Whittaker & K. Hopkins (1983, London)

Thevenot, C., *Histoire de la Bourgogne Ancienne* (1981, Dijon)

Vandyke Price, P., Alsace Wines (1984, London)

Waddell, H., Medieval Latin Lyrics (1929, London)

Warner, H., A History of Wine (1961, London)

Williams, D.A., Consideration of the Sub-Fossil Remains of Vitis-vinifera, as Evidence for Viticulture in Roman Britain, *in Britannia* (1977)

Chapter Seven

Barty-King, H., Tradition of English Wine (1977, London)

Baynes, N.H. & Moss, H., Byzantium (1948, Oxford)

Dion, R., *La Creation du Vignoble Bordelais* (1952, Anger)

Enjalbert, H., Great Bordeaux Wines: St-Emilion, Pomerol and Fransac (1985, Paris)

Francis, A.D., The Wine Trade (1972, London)

Ginestet, B., *Margaux* (1984, Paris)

Gonzalez-Gordon, N. M., Sherry, the Noble Wine (1972, London)

Harding, V., The Port of London in the 14th Century: its Topography, Administration and Trade {Doctorial thesis} (1983, St. Andrews)

Jeffs, J., Sherry (1982, London)

Johnson, H., Vintage: The Story of Wine (1989, New York)

Mackay, A., Spain in the Middle Ages (1977, London)

Livermore, H.V., A New History of Portugal (1976, Cambridge)

Newett, M. M., Canon Pietro Casola's Pilgrimage to Jerusalem in the Year 1494 (1970, Manchester)

Penning-Rowsell, E., The Wines of Bordeaux (1969, London)

Prawer, J., Colonisation Activities in the Latin Kingdom of Jerusalem, in *Revue Belge de Philologie et Histoire* (1951)

Read, J., Wines of Spain (1982, London)
— Wines of Portugal (1982, London)

Richard, J., *Croises, Missionnaires et Voyageurs* (1983, London)

Simon, A.L., The History of the Wine Trade in England (1906-9, London)

Vassberg, D., Land and Society in Golden Age Castile (1984, Cambridge)

Wilbraham, A., The Englishman's Food (1957. London)

Chapters Eight and Nine

Adams, L.D., The Wines of America (1985, New York)

Ambrosi, H. & Becker, H., *Der Deutsche Wein* (1978, Munich)

Ames, R., The Search after Claret (1961, London)

Barry, E., Observations Historical, Critical and Medical on the Wines of the Ancients (1775, London)

Barty-King, H., Tradition of English Wine (1977, Oxford)

Benwell, W.S., Journey to Wine in Victoria (1960, Carlton)

Bishop, G.C., Australian Wine-Making, the Roseworthy Influence (1988, Adelaide)

de Blij, H., Wine Regions of the Southern Hemisphere (1985, Totowa, NJ)

Bonal. F., *Le Levre d'Or de Champagne* (1984, Lausanne)

Bradford, S., The Story of Port, the Englishman's Wine (1983, London)

Braudel, F., The Structure of Everyday Life (1981, London)

Brindley, J.H., The History and Commerce of Coffee (1926, London)

Burman, J., Wine of Constantia (1979, Cape Town)

Charleston, R.J., English Glass and the Glass Used in England Circa 400-1940 (1984, London)

Charpentier, L., *Le Mystère du Vin* (1981, Paris)

Cooper, M., The Wines and Vineyards of New Zealand (1985, Auckland)-

Cossart, N., Madeira (1984, London)

Crawford, A., Bristol and the Wine Trade (1984, Bristol)

Cuny, H., Louis Pasteur (1965, London)

De Jongh, F., Encylopaedia of South African Wine (1981, Durban)

Delamain, R., *Histoire du Cognac* (1935, Paris)

Dumbrell, R., Understanding Antique Wine Bottles (1983, Suffolk)

Eisinger, J., Lead and Wine: Eberhard Gockel and the Colica Pictonum in *Medical History* (1982)

Evans, L. et al, Complete Book of Australian Wine (1978, Sydney)

Faith, N., The Story of Champagne (1988, London)
— The Winemasters (1978. London)

Fisher, H.E.S., The Portugal Trade 1700-1770 (1971, London)

Forbes, P., Champagne (1967, London)

Francis, A.D., The Wine Trade (1972, London)

Forbes, P., Champagne (1967, London)

Francis, A.D., The Wine Trade (1972, London)

Gandilhon, R., *Naissance du Champagne* (1968, Paris)

Godfrey, E.S., The Development of English Glassmaking 1560-1640 (1975, Oxford)

Gunyon, R.E.H., The Wines of Central and South-Eastern Europe (1971, London)

Halasz, Z., The Book of Hungarian Wines (1981, Budapest)

Halliday, J., The Australian Wine Companion (1985, Sydney)

Haraszthy, A., Grape Culture, Wines and Winemaking (1862, New York)

Henderson, A., The History of Ancient and Modern Wines (1824, London)

Higounet, C., *Histoire de Bordeaux* (1980, Toulouse)

Hyams, E., Dionysus: A Social History of the Vine (1965, London)

Halasz, Z., The Book of Hungarian Wines (1981, Budapest)

Higounet, C., *Histoire de Bordeaux* (1980, Toulouse)

Isnard, H., *La Vigne en Algerie* (1955, Gap)

Jeffs, J., Sherry (1982, London)

Komoroczy, G., *Borkivitelunk Eszak Fel* (1944, Kassa/Kosice)

Lachiver, M., *Vins, Vignes et Vignerons* (1988, Paris)

Lake, M., Classic Wines of Australia (1967, Melbourne)

Lausanne, E., The Great Wine Book, (1970, New York)

Linehan, M., Why You Should Buy, Drink, and Invest in Chinese Wine, https://Fontera.net/news/asia (2017)

Loubere, L., The Red and the White (1978, New York)

Macauly, R., They Came to Portugal (1946- London)

Mariacher, G., Italian Blown Glass from Ancient Rome to Venice (1961, London)

McKearin, R.H., Notes on Stopping, Bottling and Binning, in Journal of Glass

Studies (1971)

Murdoch, T. (ed), The Quiet Conquest (1985, London)

Murray Brown, R., "The Sleeping Giant," *Wine and Spirit International*, (Dec. 1992)

Olney, R., *Yquem* (1985, Paris)

Petersson, R.T., Sir Kenelm Digby: The Ornament of England (1956, London)

Pigott, S., Life Beyond Liebfraumilch (1988, London)

Redding, C., A History and Description of Modern Wines (1833, London)

Rhodes, A., Princes of the Grape (1975, London)

Roberts, L., The Merchants' Mappe of Commerce (1638, Amsterdam)

Ruggles-Brise, S.M.E., Sealed Bottles (1949, London)

Simon, A., The History of Champagne (1962, London)
— Port (1934, London)

Shaw, L.M.E., The Anglo-Portuguese Alliance and the English Merchants in Portugal 1654-1810 (1998, New York)

Smith, A., The Wealth of Nations (1776, London)

Smith. J. A., Memoirs of the Marquis of Pombal (1843, London)

Stevenson, T., Champagne (1968, London)

Sutcliffe, S., A Celebration of Champagne (1988, London)

Szabo, J. & Torok, S., Album of the Tokay-Hegyalja (1867, Tokaji)

Tchelistcheff, A., Grapes, Wine and Ecology (an interview by R. Teiser & C. Harroun) (1983, Berkeley)

De Treville, L.R., (ed), Jefferson and Wine (1989, Virginia)

Vizetelly, H., Facts About Port and Madeira (1880, London)

Willmott, H., A History of Glassmaking in England (2004, Stroud)

Wynne-Thomas, R.J.L., Relics of the Marsala Wine Trade, in *The Connoisseur* (1975)

Young, A., Travels During the Years 1787, 1788, and 1789 (1792, Bury St Edmunds)

John J. Mahoney is a Certified Wine Educator and a Literature Professor. He is Chancellor of the Dionysian Society International, a member of the American Wine Society, a Chevalerie du Verre Galant (Knights of Cognac), President of New Jersey Club Zinfandel, Director of the Tri-State Wine College, and the voice of "Weekend Wine Tips." A respected scholar of Shakespeare and Chaucer, he uses classic educational techniques when teaching about wine. He hosts corporate wine seminars, and is presently the World Ambassador for the Grand Vin wine glass series for Chef & Sommelier.

Made in the USA
Columbia, SC
17 August 2018